IN OUR VOICES, II
Stories of Holocaust Survivors

In Our Voices, II : Stories of Holocaust Survivors

Editors: Matthew Sackel and Esther Yin-Ling Spodek
Cover Design and book layout: Jason Isaac Star

86 p., 30 cm.

ISBN-13: 978-0-9816334-6-6 (pbk)
ISBN-10: 0-9816334-6-3 (pbk)

1. Holocaust, Jewish (1939-1945) — Personal narratives.
2. Skokie (Illinois).
3. Hidden Children (Holocaust).
4. Holocaust Survivors — United States.
5. Jews-Europe-Biography.
6. Jews-Illinois-Biography.

I. Title
D804.195 I5 2016

940.53/18092 B

Copyright © 2016. All rights reserved.

www.ilholocaustmuseum.org

ILLINOIS HOLOCAUST MUSEUM
& EDUCATION CENTER

TABLE OF CONTENTS

- 2 — **HOW I SURVIVED RUMBULA** | SIA HERTSBERG
- 6 — **IN THE MEMORY OF MY SISTER MARGO** | SIA HERTSBERG
- 10 — **RETURN** | SIA HERTSBERG
- 14 — **LEAVING WARSAW** | FELA DOGADKO
- 20 — **KHARKOV** | FELA DOGADKO
- 26 — **AFTER LEAVING KHARKOV** | FELA DOGADKO
- 32 — **HIDING IN THE OPEN** | PETER GERSHANOV
- 36 — **RED ARMY** | PETER GERSHANOV
- 38 — **RECOLLECTING MY LIFE** | JOE KOENIG
- 40 — **THE BALCONY OFF KASZTELANSKA STREET** | JANINE OBERROTMAN
- 42 — **THE TEACHER** | JANINE OBERROTMAN
- 46 — **THE HIDING PLACE** | JANINE OBERROTMAN
- 48 — **THE POTATO SILO** | CIPORA KATZ
- 54 — **STORIES OF MY FAMILY** | RALPH REHBOCK
- 58 — **ONE DAY AT CAMP STUTTHOF** | MARGIE OPPENHEIMER
- 62 — **OPPY** | MARGIE OPPENHEIMER
- 68 — **AUSTRALIA BOUND** | MARGIE OPPENHEIMER

Edited by
ESTHER YIN-LING SPODEK AND MATTHEW SACKEL

Designed by
JASON ISAAC STAR

FROM THE PRESIDENT | FRITZIE FRITZSHALL

Illinois Holocaust Museum & Education Center's mission has been best expressed in our founding principle: Remember the Past, Transform the Future. At the Museum, we interweave historical background with personal and intimate voices of Survivors who lived through the almost-unimaginable tragedy that is the Holocaust and later dedicated their lives to teach its history and lessons.

Story-telling is an art, and the vignettes shared in this book are the outcome of a group of Survivors and Museum staff gathered together for an ongoing writing workshop, which allowed them to craft a piece, share reactions and edits, and strengthen the telling.

The stories speak to the power of memory and are only a few of the millions that could have been written. My story is one of loss and survival. I was told upon passing through the gates of Auschwitz-Birkenau at the age of 13 to say, "I am 15." Those three simple words saved my life.

Each story is important in its own right, and together they form a powerful depiction of survival and courage, of hope and persistence.

In this new edition of *In Our Voices*, several of the authors have reflected on their stories, first printed in 2009, the year our beautiful Museum opened. Now, several authors have written a short note to their younger self. They were asked, "What would you say to the child you wrote about in this book? What words of advice or encouragement would you have given?" Two authors are no longer with us, and their families have contributed a remembrance.

I am thankful these authors took the time to put pen to paper to make this memoir and to create this legacy.

~ February 2016

FOREWORD | ESTHER YIN-LING SPODEK

January. I am walking my dog along the icy piles of old snow toward the business district of my neighborhood. I walk to the corner of Green Bay Road and Central Street, a busy intersection with a stoplight. There is an art restorer on the north side of the street. I've walked past the shop for years. But until I began to work with the Survivor's Writing Workshop, I didn't know about the woman inside. When she was four, she lived in a hole in the ground, a potato silo, in a forest in Poland, hiding from the Nazis. She was there for almost two years. Now, a retired nurse and a grandmother, she and her husband restore paintings in my neighborhood. On the first Wednesday of each month, another Survivor comes to give her a ride to the writing workshop. This man, thanks to the help of a quick-thinking stranger, got on a train different from the one that would have taken him and his mother to a concentration camp, and he was able to come to America.

Then there are the two women in the writing workshop who used to talk regularly on the phone, an employment counselor and a seamstress, but had never met in person. One was from Warsaw and one from Riga. They saw each other for the first time last year when they joined the workshop to write their Holocaust survival stories. The counselor survived by taking on a false identity as a non-Jew, and living in the open in Poland and Germany. As a girl in the Riga ghetto, one night, the seamstress fixed her pajamas with a safety pin. Later in the same night, the pin prevented a soldier from undoing her clothes and subsequently assaulting her.

In 1939, a little girl and her mother, traveled through the Soviet Union, escaping the war in Warsaw. They finally settled in Uzbekistan where the mother supported them in farm collectives until the end of the war. She is writing her story for her children and grandchildren.

Because of them, I have significant markers in my life now. When I eat potatoes, or ice cream, or when I use a safety pin or a teakettle, I remember the stories that these people have written down. These things, small items, or food that was significant to them, are triggers to the memories of specific things that happened to them.

Some years ago, when I was in my twenties and first married, my husband and I met his brother and his wife and her parents for dinner in Chinatown. It was winter and snowing in the dark streets of the south side of Chicago. They had driven in from the Indiana suburbs, and my husband and I had come from Evanston for the evening. Over dinner we listened to stories of growing up in Hungary and living in Indiana after the war, where my brother-in-law's mother-in-law, Vera, came after surviving the concentration camps. But something was missing. "I will never tell my children about what I went through during the Holocaust," she said. As her daughter sat nearby with tears on her face, Vera said, "I can't."

Many Survivors cannot speak about the Holocaust. We are lucky to have this community of writers who are willing to put down their experiences in Europe during World War II, and who are able to sit around a table with their own stories and discuss the writing with each other, and even take them home to rewrite. These stories provide an important link for us to the past, even a poignant connection to horrors in the world's recent past, in Cambodia, Bosnia, Rwanda, and Darfur, in our attempt to prevent atrocities from happening again.

It is not only for the families of women like Vera that we meet and discussed the stories these Survivors bring to the writing workshop, and not only for the families of the members of the workshop, although they provided the initial impetus to write. The members of the Survivors writing workshop have something important to tell the world, their own histories. What I have realized from reading, listening, and discussing the stories with these Survivors, is that we are all human, and in our humanity, out of horror, we can continue to live, to build families, to find satisfaction and even joy out of our lives. That we can create a viable writers community.

~June 2009

HOW I SURVIVED RUMBULA | SIA HERTSBERG

On July 1, 1941, the Nazis entered Riga.

In September, we were forced to move into a ghetto. The Nazis took one of the poorest neighborhoods and built a fence around it with a gate. All the gentiles in the neighborhood had to move out, and all the Jews who lived in Riga were told to move in. So my father, Ruvin; my mother, Katja; my little sister, Margo, who was seven; and I carried our beds, a table, four chairs, and our clothes to the neighborhood. I was fourteen years old.

Pasha, Sia on left, Margo on right.

REFLECTION : SIA HERTSBERG

You will see, you will have a happy and fulfilling life, but every day you will remember the painful memories of the Holocaust. You will keep it to yourself until one day your grandson changes everything — he encourages you to share your story with the world, and with him. And he, like you, will never forget. You must always do your best, no matter what.

We had carried our belongings out of our home the day before. My father had gone into the ghetto and found a room for us in an apartment in the only five story building in the ghetto. It was on Lacplesa Street close to the corner of Maskavas Street. The room was on the third floor in a four-room apartment. When you entered the apartment from the staircase, ours was the first room to the right. In the room next to ours lived a family of four. The father was in a wheelchair. Their last name was Vovsi. A young couple by the name of Jaffe lived in the third room. The oldest son from the Vovsi family lived in the little maid's room off the kitchen.

Since all of Riga was occupied, entire German families moved into our old apartments outside of the ghetto. Our men were taken to forced labor factories each day and brought back in the evening. Our women were allowed to go looking for work with the German families now living in our homes. They would hire us to be their cleaning ladies for pocket change. Since the homes and apartments outside of the ghetto were heated, it was considered lucky if you could find a job there. None of the apartments in the ghetto were heated. My mother and sister could not find jobs, but I was one of the lucky. If you had a job, then you had to be escorted out of the ghetto by a German. The husband of the family I worked for was named Fritz, and his wife was named Johana. During the days when I did not have work, I stayed in the apartment with my mother, my sister, Mrs. Jaffe, Mrs. Vovsi, and her wheelchair-bound husband.

Sometimes people were able to smuggle in food from their gentile friends if they had jobs outside the ghetto. I can remember returning at the end of the day to the ghetto and seeing our gentile nanny, Pasha. Pasha would come to the fence to try to bring us food. She would come to meet me at the gate with bread that I would smuggle into the ghetto for the rest of my family. Our street was the last street along the border of the ghetto, so it was divided in half, with one half for the Jewish ghetto and one half for the gentiles. The fence separating the ghetto from the rest of Riga was on this last street, so we faced the gentiles living there.

On November 29, the men were taken to forced labor as usual. We had no idea in the morning that the men would not be brought back. As day continued and the men still had not returned, rumors began circulating that we were going to be resettled in a different location. We started to prepare ourselves for the coming journey. We sewed three backpacks according to our ability to carry them. My sister had a very small one since she was only seven. My mother and I made our backpacks bigger.

Nobody could guess that the next morning we would all be killed in the Rumbula forest. Writing it now, after sixty-seven years, I am feeling sick. When the men did not return, we knew it was a bad sign. It was about midnight when we prepared and packed our backpacks. Mother told us to go to bed. Who knew when they would wake us up? We washed ourselves, and my sister and I put on our pajamas. The elastic in my pajama pants broke. I found a safety pin. To this day, I can remember the pajamas. They were red with narrow white stripes. I have every detail of that night in my memory forever.

Mother told me, "Forget about your elastic, just go to bed." So I decided to fasten my pants in the back with the safety pin. We went to bed a few minutes after midnight. Noises woke us up just after two o'clock, shouting in the stairways and knocking on the doors with the guns. When we opened the door, four Latvians with guns in their hands were yelling, "Out, right out, and fast!" They were wearing German uniforms. I recognized one of them from school. I had attended Latvian School No. 47 until the Germans came. He was two years older than me, so he had to have been sixteen. One of the Latvians, probably the chief, a man about thirty years old, short, wearing the brown German uniform, said, "I will have her." He grabbed me by the shoulder and pushed me into our room, the first room to the right. The room was crowded with our three beds. He threw me on the bed closest to the door. I knew and understood very clearly that after he had me, he would shoot me. At that moment I was no longer a child.

In my mind I had nothing to lose. I told myself to fight. With his right hand he held a pistol to my temple, and pinned my left arm underneath his forearm. With his left hand he opened his pants and tried to pull down my pajamas. But the safety pin kept him from getting my pants down. I scratched him with my right hand and bit and screamed. I knew that after a minute I would lose my fight. But at that moment, the boy I recognized from the school saved me. He ran in and screamed "Priekšnieka k-gs atvainojiet bet židi šauj," which meant, "Chief, excuse me, but the Jews are shooting."

They both ran out. My mother closed the door and told us, "Let them shoot us right here. We are not going anyplace." Later on, my mother told me there could not possibly have been Jews shooting. Jews did not have guns. The schoolboy made it up to save me.

While I had been fighting for my life, the Vovsis took Mr. Vovsi on a stretcher and left. The wheelchair was still in the apartment. I was still on the bed, constantly making it wet and shaking. I was completely numb and could not get up. My mother and my sister were sitting next to me. They were also shaking. They were trying to comfort me. We could hear the Latvians shouting "Ara, ara, visi, ara, atrak," which means "Out, out, everybody out, fast." Suddenly the washroom door opened. Mrs. Jaffe fell through the door and fainted. My mother and sister got her up and told her, "We are not going. Let them shoot us right here."

We could hear shooting going on outside, but Mrs. Jaffe was scared and told us that she was going to leave. My mother told her she could not leave while there was still screaming in the staircase. She told her to wait until it was quiet. My mother did not want the Latvians to find us. We were on the third floor, so there were two floors above us and two below. We heard screaming up and down the stairs, above and below us.

My mother made Mrs. Jaffe wait until everything was quiet and she was sure there were no more Latvians on the stairs. We could hear their footsteps. They were still knocking on the doors with their guns. After a while it became quiet inside the building. Eventually, my mother let Mrs. Jaffe leave. She left only to be shot in the Rumbula forest with the rest of the elderly, the women, and the children. The men never returned from the factory.

At about five o'clock in the morning, we started hearing terrible noises on the street behind the fence outside of the ghetto. They were screaming on the street, "Atrak, atrak," faster, faster. My mother and sister went to the bedroom window. Because of the war rules, all the windows had been covered with black covers. My mother made a tiny hole to see through. We thought that maybe the Russians had come and people were screaming "Hurrah, hurrah," but that is not what it was. My mother and sister saw the Latvians in SS uniforms. They were on horses. They pushed women, children, babies, and elderly people who could hardly walk, hitting them and screaming "Atrak, atrak," faster, faster. Faster to Rumbula, to the grave. Jews were running to Rumbula to be shot into mass graves. At that moment, no one knew where they were going, to the mass graves in the Rumbula forest, already dug for them.

When they got to the mass graves, the Latvians told them to undress. They were told to make three separate piles: shoes, clothes, and coats. Years later I realized why so many could not fight back or run away. The shame and humiliation of their nakedness prevented them from moving. The Jews were forced to line up in rows of six. They were shot. They all fell into the mass graves. Then the soldiers lined up another six to be shot.

We know what happened in the Rumbula forest only because one woman survived. The bullets missed her, but she fell into the grave anyway. She crawled out of the mass grave the next morning. Her last name was Medalje. She escaped and was hidden by some good Latvians. She died in 2002 in Riga. She was the lone Survivor of the Rumbula massacre.

The rounding up and killing of large groups was called an "action." The SS and the Latvians had divided the ghetto for the first shooting on November 29, and then a second action on December 8. Thirty thousand of Riga's Jews were killed on those two dates in Rumbula Forest.

We stayed in our apartment, quiet like mice, till the second action was over. Then there was a command to stop shooting. The big ghetto was now empty. A smaller ghetto took its place. The time between the two actions and the setting up of the smaller ghetto is lost in my memory. After the second action we could probably hear some people returning to the streets, so we left our apartment. I cannot remember actually leaving the apartment. The SS were looking for seamstresses, and I told them I was a seventeen-year-old seamstress so that I could get a job again.

The safety pin saved my life. That night will stay in front of my eyes for the rest of my life. After that we ended up with seventy-five others in the city. I don't remember how we got from the apartment. We were taken by the Reichskommissariat, Germans in brown uniforms. My mother, sister, and I lived in a workshop. I was a seamstress and my mother was a cleaning lady. We hid my little sister.

*Fourth grade class picture.
Natalie (front row, second from left)
and Sia (front row, fourth from left).*

IN THE MEMORY OF MY SISTER MARGO | SIA HERTSBERG

Sia's sister, Margo, pre-war.

How did we get to that point, to forty-seven pounds?

I was born in Riga, Latvia in 1927. Between 1941 and 1944, I survived the Riga ghetto, then the Kasernierung, a building where we lived and worked, and then two concentration camps, Kaiserwald and the Truppenwirtschaftslager, both in Riga. I was in the ghetto with my mother, father, and sister from September 30, 1941 until about December 15, 1941. The Kasernierung was at Reichskommissariat and was located on the corner of Kalku and Valnu Streets. There were seventy-five people in the building, tailors and dressmakers. I was a dressmaker. My mother was a cleaning woman and my sister was hiding. My father was also there. This was from the end of December 1941 until about the end of 1943, or the beginning of 1944.

We were sent to Kaiserwald and were there for about a week. Then we were separated from my father. My mother, sister, and I were sent to the Truppenwirtschaftslager. In this camp the Nazis brought us uniforms that had to be fixed and cleaned.

On September 24, 1944, my forty-three-year-old mother, ten-year-old sister, Margo, and I were pushed onto a boat named the Kanonier. We were with about three thousand remaining Jews, those who were still left in Riga after massive shootings by Germans and Latvians. We were thrown into a hole from the main deck of the boat. There was sand on the very bottom. It was very dark. There were no bathrooms, so all of us, men and women, used the same pails. We were given neither food nor water. People were getting seasick. We sat in a sandy pool of urine, feces, and vomit for about three or four days as the boat crossed the Baltic Sea.

When we arrived in Danzig, Poland we were put on a train. We were shoved into narrow rail cars. There were no windows or doors. The ones who got pushed on first did not survive because they were crushed by people pushed on after them. On October 1, we arrived at Stutthof als Vernichtungslager, a death camp.

We were forced to undress ourselves and then were given striped gray and blue dresses and wooden shoes. My sister's feet were too small for the wooden clogs, so the German SS man told her to keep her own shoes. I still have all three identifications from Stutthof, signed by my mother, my sister, and myself. These identification papers show our prisoner numbers on them. My prisoner number was 93927. My mother's prisoner number was 93929. My sister's prisoner number was 93928.

My mother, sister, and I were placed in Barrack 19. There were two Russian women in charge of the barrack, Shura and her assistant, Tanja. They would frequently beat the prisoners, even killing some of them. They would not let us use the lavatory or wash. When Shura and Tanja yelled "Out!" we had to be outside immediately or we would be beaten or shot. They called us out for appell, where we lined up to be counted. This happened at least twice a day. During this time we were humiliated and forced to do exercises. If someone could not bend as fast as the SS wanted her to, she was shot on the spot. Tanja and Shura screamed, "Bend! Get up! Bend! Get up!" and in between their shouts we could hear them laughing. They often had big German shepherd dogs with them. I can still hear them screaming and the dogs barking.

Twice a day we were told to go outside, and four people were given a bowl of black water to share. We took turns taking sips. In the morning we were each given a piece of bread. This one piece of bread had to last the whole day. We were never given any other food. One day there was a dead horse outside the barracks. After being counted, we ran to the dead horse and pulled it apart with our hands so we could eat the meat from inside the dead horse.

We slept four people sitting on a plank. The planks were three levels high. We would sit with our knees pulled into our chest. We were also attacked by lice because we were never allowed to wash ourselves. We would fight the lice, something we could never do with the SS or Russian women who beat us. We would pinch the lice between our nails and listen to them cracking. But they continued to multiply. They outnumbered us, and we could not do better winning a battle against the lice than we could against the armed SS with their rifles, dogs, and boots.

Typhus broke out in the camp in January. People were dying all the time. The ones who were still alive had to carry the dead people in blankets to the crematoriums where there were mountains of dead people. We had to keep piling up the dead bodies. Then they were put into crematoriums where they were burned.

Soon my sister and I caught the fever that comes with typhus. We were dying of thirst as we sat on the top wooden plank in the barracks. There were no more appells. My sister and I became too weak and too sick to move. My mother still had to carry dead bodies back and forth. It was winter, and even though it was cold, my sister and I were burning up with fever. There was snow outside. My sister and I were both so sick that we were ready to die. My mother said to me, "I am going to get some snow," so that we would have something to drink. When she returned she did not have her can with her. She told me that when she got outside and bent down to put some snow in her can, an SS man kicked her in the head. She soon lost consciousness there on the top wooden plank. That is where she died on February 7, 1945.

I made sure that I would always remember the day my mother died. I did this by taking a comb and breaking off two teeth on the left side marking the second month, February, and seven teeth from the right side of the comb to remember the day. Then four people came into our barracks, and I told them that my mother was dead. It took all four of them to carry her out. They were like walking skeletons themselves.

March arrived and Margo and I had to go on a death march from Stutthof. We didn't know where we were going. In that moment, we did not know it was a death march. We thought we were being sent to a different location. We did not know anything. We were just walking, day and night. The death march lasted three days. I still had my wooden shoes. Margo was still wearing her leather boots. They were too small. The winter weather froze her feet. As we walked, my sister told me she could no longer go on, but I told her we had to or we would be shot. The SS shot anyone who stopped walking. At one point she begged me to stop, so I finally did. We stopped in a ditch. I can still see that dark ditch where I sat with my sister. I felt that either we would both live or we would both die. We lowered our heads and waited to be shot. Then, suddenly, I heard two shots. I picked up my head and there was an SS soldier standing there shooting, into the air and not at us. He looked at me and said, "Mein Got solche kleine kinder." My God, such little children. Then he left.

Eventually we began walking again. Everyone left. I forced my sister to get up, and we went to the nearest house. There were three steps to the house. We crawled on all fours up those three steps. We knocked on the door. Some Polish people let us into their kitchen. They gave us each a glass of milk, a piece of bread, and a hamburger, but we could not even swallow what we ate. I begged the Polish family to save us and hide us. I told them that we had money in the United States and that we would pay them. But they said the Germans would kill them if they found us there, and they showed us the way to the concentration camp.

That evening we walked by ourselves to the concentration camp where the others were. When we got there no one was even at the gate. We were at Camp Burgraben, Poland, our final destination. We thought it was the end of our lives, another camp of death like the one we had just left. But there were no beds in the barracks, just straw on the floor. We lay on the straw and did not move. In the morning, when the sun came through the windows, I could see lice everywhere in the straw. They were so tiny, like fleas. We could not even feel them as they ate us alive. We were too ill even to fight with tiny lice. We just lay there. I do not know how many days I spent on that floor listening helplessly to my little sister Margo, who screamed from the pain of her frostbite. We were all moaning and dying, and the smell of dead bodies quickly filled the barracks.

On March 23 the Russian army stormed into our barracks, and upon seeing us, they called for stretchers. The Russian soldiers started to weep when they looked at us. What were they seeing? Our skin barely covered our bones. They undressed us because the rags we were wearing were covered with lice. They put blankets on us. They asked us our first and last names, where we were born, our ages, and finally if we were men or women. We were emaciated. Our skin color had turned dark brown. The soldiers could not even tell if they were talking to a man or a woman. We must not have looked human. Finally, they put us on stretchers. Some people died even as they were being placed on the stretchers. Death came all the time, on the wooden planks, while standing and being counted, while walking, while on the straw, while being put on stretchers.

Margo and I were taken to a schoolhouse that had been turned into a hospital by the Russians. It was on Falkweig Street in the city of Langfurh. The soldiers were crying as they carried us. I was seventeen years old. I remember being weighed in the hospital. I was forty-seven pounds. How could I get to that point, to forty-seven pounds, and still be alive?

Margo died in my arms at that hospital. It was gangrene that took her life. She was all that I had left. It was night, and there was a Russian nurse named Shura. She squeezed my right arm and woke me. "Your sister is dying," she said.

We were in two beds that had been pushed together. I looked over and I could see that her eyes were still open. She lifted her hand to wave good-bye at me, but no words left her mouth. Her eyes closed, and now she was dead. My baby sister was gone forever. They took my baby sister and buried her on a hill behind the school.

In May, I was told that I was going to be sent on a train back home. I was still too weak to walk. I had to be carried on a stretcher by two Russian soldiers. Before they put me on the train, I asked to see where my sister was buried. They took me to a hill behind the school/hospital and I saw many graves there. Each had a marker on it. My sister's marker said:

Israilevich, Margo
Born October 3rd, 1934
Died April 21, 1945

In 2002 I traveled to see the camp, now the Museum of Stutthof. The director, Janina Grabowska, showed me a map of the road where we made our death march. She told me that the death march had lasted three-to-four days and she pointed to the school where Margo died. It is now the French Lyceum. I had come to look for my sister's grave. When I got there I did not find the grave or the stick that had marked the grave. Now there was only asphalt, not even one marker to identify it as the place where my sister and the other liberated camp Survivors were buried. My story will have to be the marker for the graves of my sister and my mother. I took photos of all the things I saw in 2002 so I could show what was left of all that I endured. And I will share the pictures to tell my story.

Sia's sister, Margo.

...we could not even swallow what we ate.

RETURN | SIA HERTSBERG

Sia's passport photo.

For many years, I wanted to go back and see the concentration camp where I was interned during World War II.

However, I procrastinated because I knew it would be very emotional and difficult for me. Finally, because I felt I had to, I returned in July of 2002.

My Polish friend, Adam, helped motivate me to finally make the trip. Although I had met Adam while he was working in the United States, he had since returned to his native Poland, where he was permanently residing. Adam had gone to the Stutthof Museum for me in 1996 because he knew I wanted to get information and documents showing that I had been a prisoner in the camp. He met the museum's director, Janina Grabowska. She was able to find three original documents signed by my mother, my sister, and me upon our admission to the camp. She gave them to Adam, who also made a videotape of the camp while he was there.

Adam came to the United States with the papers and the video and delivered them to me personally. After I saw the papers, I could not sleep, eat, or talk for three days and nights. After those three days I watched the video. But it was the papers with my mother's and sister's signatures and our prisoner numbers that upset me the most. Everything came back to me. Holding the papers made me decide to go back and see everything for myself, to recall the details gone from my memory and to inspire people to actively remember what had happened to us.

In July 2002 I went to Poland. Adam and his wife, Mila, met me at the Krakow airport. There were only about two hundred Jewish people living in Krakow at this time, but before the war the town was one quarter Jewish. Adam lived close to Krakow in a nearby suburb. Krakow is on the south end of Poland, and Gdansk (Danzig), with the remains of the Stutthof concentration camp, is on the north end of Poland. We had to travel a week by car to go across Poland. During the entire trip I tape-recorded myself speaking in English. I was so nervous and I was afraid that I might not remember everything. My neighbor, Donna Guilley, transcribed my tape-recorded notes when I returned. We sat in her apartment and listened to my voice narrating my own journey.

Coming close to Stutthof. It is July 23, 2002, a Tuesday. I feel like throwing up. Very scary; it seems very scary to me. Coming close, I miss my children. I miss my grandchildren. And, I miss very much Simon (my long-term companion who passed). Adam and Mila support me very much and they are beautiful people but I do miss my children, really. I see the fence and I remember how they were taking us. I was holding my little sister's hand and my mother was on the other side. They were taking us there and taking everything away from us. They were undressing us and taking our clothes, shoes, everything. They gave us the striped suits (a dress and a jacket) and wooden shoes to wear. (My sister was allowed to keep her leather shoes due perhaps to her youth and beauty.) So, we are walking. On my right side is a forest and on the left side is the camp. I don't recognize it. I don't recognize anything. It is very different from the way it was in 1944. Today there are flowers and trees planted at the gates.

In Stutthof, my sister Margo and I were admitted into Block 19. This occurred on October 3, 1944. I will never forget the date because it was Margo's tenth birthday. All who survived the terrible boat trip from Riga to Danzig surely remember that the very young and the very old stood no chance. To stay together, we altered our ages and abilities. We all got in lines and had to give our names, ages, and professions or how educated we were, and which languages we could speak. I said I was born in 1926 instead of 1927, and Margo also lied about her age. We knew they were killing younger children and older people, so my mother made herself younger while we made ourselves older. I said I was a seamstress. No one had any documents for the SS men to check. The SS men recording the information also wrote down the color of our eyes. We had already had our heads shaved by this time. That was how I arrived in Stutthof for the first time.

When I arrived at Stutthof for the second time, I was with my Polish friends Adam and Mila. Now it was a museum in memory of the concentration camp I had survived. I sat with Janina for three hours and found out a lot of things I had forgotten. I learned that the death march lasted for three days and nights. I could not recall how long it had taken for us to go from one concentration camp to another. However, I could easily recall how hard it was to march so far in such cold temperatures, my little sister Margo saying that she could go no further, and how I pleaded with her to continue, knowing we would be shot if we sat or fell down.

As I sat with Janina, I also thought about how my mother was not with us during the march. Her life had already been taken by the hand and foot of a German SS after she attempted to get snow for her children to "drink." My mother had gone outside the barrack with a little kettle to get some snow because Margo and I were burning up with fevers and dying of thirst. As she bent over, an SS man kicked the kettle out of her hand and then kicked her in the head with his heavy boot. She came back to the top wooden plank where Margo and I were laying and told us that an SS man had kicked away her kettle and then kicked her in the head. She lost consciousness soon after and never woke up again. Three days later she was dead. She was forty-three years old when she was killed. That is why she was not on the death march with us.

Janina was able to look at maps and show me the actual route we had walked on that death march. I began to think about the ditch where Margo and I might have been killed. It had become too difficult for my little sister to keep walking, and I would never leave her. Eventually, Margo simply could not go on, so we lay in a ditch. I was expecting us to be shot, but the SS man who looked right at us shot into the air and left. When he was gone, Margo and I crawled across the road and made it to a nearby house. The people who lived there gave us some food, which made us sick after having not eaten in so long. We begged them to hide us but they were afraid to keep us there. They told us how to get to another camp, Burgraben, about fifty kilometers from Stutthof. We did not know what else to do, and we were afraid of being shot with our striped dresses and bald heads, so we went to this camp. It turned out to be the final destination of the death march we had just left. On the way, the road was littered with the dead bodies of other prisoners.

When we arrived at Burgraben there was no one at the gate. Margo and I collapsed on lice-ridden straw. On March 23, 1945, the Russian army saved us. They brought us to a school being used as a hospital. Many people died there, including my sister. Janina called some elders in the region and found a ninety-year-old man who remembered the "hospital." She did this so we could easily find it after leaving the museum. The school is now called Lyceum IB 1309 World School. The city and street have been updated from Langfurh, Falkweig to Gdansk Wrzeszcz, Topolova.

Adam, Mila, and I continued our journey in search of the roads I traveled during the death march, the Burgraben camp, and the hospital where Margo died. My taped voice speaks back to me:

We will make some more kilometers today but I don't think we will make it all the way to the other camp, Burgraben, because it is too far. We will go back to the hotel and tomorrow we will go the other way to see Burgraben and then we will go [to] the place where the hospital was. The Russians placed all the liberated people in this hospital because none of us were able to stand on our feet. I was close to eighteen years old, my weight was twenty-five [kilograms]. My sister Margo was ten and had gangrene in her legs. At the Stutthof Museum I was told the Russians burned the camp down after the liberation because of the lice and unsanitary conditions.

The next day:

Today is July 24th, 2002. We continue the trip to where my sister and I marched in 1945. The road is narrow, it is a two-way road with houses on one side some of the time. I don't remember the road at all. It has been moved and completely redone. There are new houses and, as you can imagine, it is impossible for me to remember because of the condition I was in. I had typhus and I was taking my ten-year-old sister, who had the frostbite in her legs, by the hand. We were able to find the road only because it had been very clearly pointed out to us at the museum. We will finish the road today.

The next stop was Burgraben. There we found a small monument made of stone but no museum as in Stutthof. We got to look around the camp. It was a massive place but only one part remains undisturbed. The wires are still there, but nothing else. In Polish, the monument reads:

For all Prisoners of Stutthof Death Camp in Kokoszki
Forever Glory and Remembrance
Who Were Tortured And Killed by the Nazi People-killers
In the Years 1944-1945

There was nothing there. The three of us stood there in the forest. I sat in front of the monument and Adam took my picture. I look back now and realize there were fresh flowers on this monument in the middle of forest that was once a camp of death, in a place where there are no more Jewish people living. I wonder who left those fresh flowers.

My notes continued, as we approach the school/hospital: "And there [it] is right like I remembered, like I was telling always. Uh, a little like a, not a mountain but, uh, like a mountain." I was so emotional that I temporarily lost my ability to use English and could not retrieve the word "hill." Although the hill where Margo was buried is still there, the marker that acted as a headstone is gone. It used to read:

Israilevich, Margo
Born October 3, 1934
Died April 21, 1945

We were at the school in July and no one was there except a cleaning lady. We gave her money to so she would let us in. We asked where the back door was that would lead us to the hill where I knew my sister was buried. We told her that in 1945 this building had been made into a hospital for Jewish Survivors from concentration camps. She said that she had not been working back then, but pointed to an old man, the janitor, and she called him over. When he came to where we were standing, Adam asked him in Polish if he knew anything about the school being used as a hospital for Jewish Survivors during the war. The man became angry and said that he did not know anything about Jews. He yelled at the cleaning lady for letting us in. Soon, two young boys, about seventeen years old, showed up. They were carrying big tree branches like weapons. Adam and Mila squeezed me in between them and said, "Let's go." We left. We gave the cleaning lady some extra money and thanked her.

Our journey lasted about eight days, and then I returned to Adam and Mila's house near Krakow. I was with them for a month. They put fresh flowers in my room every day. We visited other Jewish cemeteries and saw the location where the movie Schindler's List was made. Within a week of my return to the United States, my neighbor Donna transcribed my audiotapes. I had returned to Stutthof, and then I had to return to my new home in the United States to tell my story.

Sia and her husband's wedding photo, October 07, 1946.

On the way, the road was littered with the dead bodies of other prisoners.

LEAVING WARSAW | FELA DOGADKO

I. **My upcoming fourth birthday was my family's reason to plan a big celebration. I was the third child born to my parents and the first to have lived beyond the age of two.** My great-grandma, my two grandmas, my grandpa, numerous aunts and uncles and assorted family friends had all committed to come to the party and to rejoice. Then September 1, 1939 happened, and by the time October 23 rolled in I was already far from Zelazna Str. 63, Warsaw.

There would be no birthday party.

"The Coat," Fela's gift from her grandfather upon escaping Warsaw in 1939.

REFLECTION : FELA DOGADKO

I live my second childhood now.
And since my second childhood is entirely up to me, I'd better make it a great one.
A phrase I like to repeat is: When I grow up I want to be ME.

September 1, 1939. War came to Warsaw with all of its ferociousness and savagery. The massive German airplanes crowded the sky over the city. The drone of their engines soon became alarming and frightening. Their enormous bodies hung from the sky, their elongated shadows intersecting with each other on the streets, on the buildings, and on the park benches. They spread darkness in an eerie way.

Bombs rained from the sky, and hours into the war Warsaw was on fire. The bomb fire's light was ominous. Warsaw was the city in which all of my family was born, as far back as anyone could remember or know. Now, a few peklach and zeklach, and seven of us were leaving everything familiar. The family's exodus included my Aunt Chajcie with her two-year-old daughter, Estush, my Aunt Sara-Rywka, my parents, and me. My grandpa came with us too. But my grandma did not want to leave. "I'll stay and take care of everything here for when you come back," she said. "You go with them, they'll need your help with the two babies," she urged her husband. "How long can the war possibly last? It will blow over in no time." My Grandpa Baruch eventually gave in to his wife's pleading.

Before we left, Grandpa Baruch made sure that I had a warm. The mention of Siberia must have frightened everyone. My grandpa was a designer of leather shoe uppers. The leather cutters were considered the aristocracy of the shoe-making process. He was proud of his skills and made sure that people knew the difference between being a cobbler and a design-cutter. When cutting to his design, he had to visualize how to position the pattern in order to get the most out of the leather skin. He had to be efficient and precise, and, in the instructions to the cobbler, he always included the size of my mom's shoes, so that the sample would be made in my mom's size. My mom got the sample to wear after it was shown and modeled. Sometimes she got to model the samples herself. She had beautiful legs.

My grandpa knew many people in the leather business, so he was able to find craftsmen, who, on very short notice, agreed to make a coat for a four-year-old girl. No one in the entire world, certainly not a four-year-old, had a coat like mine, I'm sure. I loved it from the minute that my grandpa presented it to me. It was just so very soft. It hugged me. The shearling coat was made of the finest sheepskin with the fur inside. The exposed fur trimmed the cuffs and the hem and the entire length of the front where leather loops closed on the buttons. The two large pockets were hand-sewn to the leather. A matching hat with earflaps and a muff completed the outfit. A wide belt was added for additional warmth, and someone in the family bought for me a pair of felt boots (perfect for frost, not for water). I was equipped for Siberia.

I said farewell to all that I had known. Farewell to Zelazna Str. 63 where my cradle stood and was now to be forever empty. Farewell to the beach on the banks of the Vistula, to the beautiful Lazienki Park, to Jerozolimski Avenue promenade, to my Aunt Dora (my mom's sister) and to my Uncle Max (my mom's youngest sibling) who stayed in Warsaw. Farewell to the best people on earth, who had surrounded me from the moment I was born. Life would never be normal from that point forward. Fall was known for its beauty in Poland, but there was nothing beautiful about it in the year 1939.

Our small group joined others who were fleeing from the only homeland they'd known. We ran toward the Polish-Russian border. We had no known destination, just a geographical direction. Eastward.

Masses of people walked bearing heavy loads of belongings and children in their arms. A few, who could afford to pay the hefty price demanded by farmers, would secure a ride in a mule cart only to be dropped off at a short distance away. There was nothing one could do about being cheated. Everyone was at the mercy of somebody else. Some people considered themselves extremely lucky when they could hitch a ride and sit on top of their salvaged possessions, and at least rest their feet for a while. Most walked till their feet bled.

Many trains were already stopped dead on the bombed out tracks, piles of mangled metal in places. Miles of railroad ties were shredded into splinters and dust.

I also walked, but mostly I was carried by my mom, my dad, or my grandpa. The chill in the air and the night dampness did not penetrate my coat. I was warm, for the most part. Still, when I was particularly fearful, or scared, or hungry, I shivered even inside this coat. No coat could insulate me from the sounds of the air raid sirens, or the booms of exploding bombs, or the sight of people whose legs buckled underneath them, and, unable to take one more step, were left in the places where they fell.

Exhausted, hungry, thirsty, and filthy, the sorrowful group of hundreds made it to the Neutral Zone, a muddy field, a strip of wasteland in the middle of nowhere. There were no sanitary facilities, nothing at all, just a place where thousands of refugees put down their belongings and waited for the Soviet Union to open its borders. The constant drizzle made the field muddier and muddier, and the soaked clothes never had a chance to dry.

Horrible news trickled in from Warsaw by way of newly arriving refugees. Warsaw was burning to ashes. Jews were being forced to abandon their homes and surrender their valuables. More and more of them were being crowded into smaller and smaller spaces. Grandpa Baruch felt guilty for leaving his wife behind, and he missed her terribly. He was unhappy and getting extremely restless. He made a decision to go back to Warsaw to share the dismal fate together with my grandma. There was nothing any one of us could do or say that would change his mind.

A man in his early fifties, tall, slim, vigorous and alert, practically overnight turned into a hunched, ancient man. I watched him move away from me carrying his bundle on his back. I cried and I waved and I called out to him, "Zayde, Zayde!" I knew that he heard me. His figure stopped for a moment, and I hoped that he would change his mind come back, but he didn't. He didn't even turn around to look at me. Not even once.

I never saw him again.

In Warsaw, Fela with her mom and grandfather, Baruch Kellerwajs, in 1937.

11. We stayed in the Neutral Zone for many more days, maybe even weeks. The rain soaked through every piece of clothing we wore, and the already muddy field became a swamp. The mud stank. The clothes stank. There wasn't a single spot where we could hide from the elements. We were on a piece of land packed with waiting refugees.

Pesa Bernstein and her mother, hearing of our predicament, came to help us. They introduced themselves to us as being from Bialystok, which was not too far from the refugee holding camp. They were among a number of other volunteers who shared food and blankets with the displaced people. It must have been on the second or third visit when Pesa told us that every time she looked at her daughter, Cywia, she saw me and couldn't get me out of her head. Eventually Pesa asked my mom to pack our clothes and come with them to their house in Bialystok, at the same time apologizing to my father, to my Aunt Chajcie with Estush, and to my Aunt Sara-Rywka for not being able to extend the offer to them also.

When I saw Cywia I could have been looking into a mirror. She was my age, exactly. She was chubby, like me. She had long, very dark brown hair, which she wore braided, just like me.

There were truly wall-to-wall people in Pesa's small apartment. People were spread out on floors and sitting on every piece of furniture. Cywia guided me through the maze to her crib and told me that I could sleep in it. She herself liked to sleep with her mama and bubbe in their big bed anyway. Her mama had told her that I had no home, and that everything had been taken away from me. This was why she wanted me to have her crib.

Pesa found a burlap potato sack, and, together with my mom, sewed a cover for my coat. According to Pesa, the coat in its original beauty would be too much of a temptation for anyone not to rip it off my back.

Within days, news came to the Bernstein family that the Soviet Union had finally opened its borders to the refugees stretched out on the field. Mom and I joined the others of our family and waited for a place in an open-bed truck to be taken into the Soviet Union.

It was mayhem. No one asked where the trucks were heading. People just hoped that they were being taken away from Poland. There was a lot of pushing and shoving, crying, and calling out of names. Would more trucks be provided? Would the border be closed again? No one was sure of anything.

At this point, parents were separated from their children, husbands from wives, sisters from brothers, and baggage from its owners. My parents and I were unusually lucky to be herded into the same truck, but Aunt Sarah was pushed into another, and Aunt Chajcie with Estush into yet another.

We were now inside the borders of the Soviet Union. In August 1939, foreign ministers Ribbentrop and Molotov signed a nonaggression pact between Germany and the Soviet Union, so Russia was placated. But I remember my mom saying that she knew that Hitler wouldn't stop at the border of Russia, and she was hoping that we could move as far as possible from the Polish-Russian border.

At least, for now, this country was at peace. The railroad tracks were still intact, and trucks were running on roads, which, though in very bad shape, were, for the most part, passable. Horse-drawn carts shared the roads with trucks, especially in smaller cities or farming communities.

We survived. My father was a tailor and his skills were portable. All he needed was a needle and thread and he was in business. Everyone everywhere had something that needed to be repaired, or let out, or a hole patched, mended, or darned. Actually, the major part of his work consisted of letting out hems.

On a new garment the hems were intentionally made very wide. They were meant to be let out and let out again as a child grew. It was not at all unusual to see two or three permanent creases around the bottom or on the cuffs of a garment. In any village or city neighborhood, someone always appeared to own a sewing machine. An iron, in which one put glowing pieces of coal, was also available here and there. My father bartered his services for a place to stay and for food to eat, and he could do it all without knowing a word of Russian.

We were afraid to stay too close to Poland, so we kept inching our way deeper and deeper into the Soviet Union. The names of two cities stand out clearly in my mind. Cherepovets and Vologda. But they were way up north and a little bit east from the Bialystok area. They seemed to be on the way to Siberia. It could have been that that's where we were being sent. That's where everybody else was being sent. That's where my Aunt Sara-Rywka was sent, we found out after the war. By sheer luck or coincidence, we made a U-turn and started heading south.

Moscow was one of the cities we stayed in for maybe a few days. Of Moscow itself I remember only the subway. The underground was so huge. It was clean, well lit, and there were many marble statues, and the walls were all covered with pretty paintings. There was no housing available in Moscow, and there was no one to turn to for help in this large city. We were very soon on the road again. Many months had passed since we had left Poland, and we were as yet to stay in one place for more than a few days or weeks.

But, whenever we established a new address, my mom would write to her parents and to her sister and brother in occupied Warsaw. I recall seeing a few letters that made it through to us. The envelopes were all marked up with numerous stamps of different sizes and colors, each with the madman's face on them. Deutschland was prominently placed on the envelope. The letters looked like jigsaw puzzles, words and entire sentences erased or cut out by censors. By the end of 1941 the letters stopped coming altogether, but this didn't stop my mom from writing and from mailing them.

Throughout the war years I sat tight by my mom's side and followed her letter writing. This is how I learned my numbers and the names of the months. I wondered why the first number on the date kept changing all the time, the second number not as fast, and the third -- never. Today, after more than forty years in the States, the month before the day does not come automatically to me.

Fela, about two and one-half years old.

Fela's father, Selik (center).

It was **mayhem**. No one asked **where** the trucks were **heading**.

KHARKOV | FELA DOGADKO

After zigzagging
through many cities large and small, we unloaded in Kharkov. In the summer of 1940, this large city was at peace. My father easily found work tailoring and we were able to afford rent for a room in a Russian family's apartment. We also had enough money for food.

Family photo before the war — Fela and her parents.

On the sidewalks of the city's wide, tree-lined boulevards, children played hopscotch and jumped ropes or just promenaded up and down the streets with their parents. The parks were full of people. Ice cream-licking kids occupied the benches. Some had suckers to lick. The suckers were in the shape of roosters, and they came in one color only, red. Flowers were all over Kharkov. On each corner a vendor would sell bunches of flowers out of buckets. Balloons were sold on the streets. It was a colorful sight. At dusk, the entire city was illuminated by the many streetlights and by the glow of lights coming from every open and unshaded window.

On the outskirts of Kharkov was a kiddie land. It occupied a very large area. The amusement park was run by the Pioneers, all dressed up in required uniforms of white shirts, red ties, and dark-colored skirts or pants. The Pioneers were the junior branch of the Communist Party.

I liked the carousel and the train best of all. The carousel's elaborately painted horses moved up and down and around. You could hear the calliope carnival music that came from the carousel throughout the park. Sounds of happily clanking train bells mixed with the sounds of frolicking and excited kids. There was a row of distorting mirrors. The reflections were so funny. People held their bellies, laughing. Some were a little bit scary to me. My parents took me to the park many times, and I always got a balloon and an ice cream cone. I didn't go on many rides because I got sick on them.

We hoped to stay in Kharkov until the war blew over. It didn't happen. One beautiful summer day everything changed. On June 22, 1941, Kiev, the capital city of the Ukraine Republic of the Soviet Union, was attacked by Germany. Kharkov, which was fewer than two hundred miles from Kiev, was put on alert. Loudspeakers were installed on major street corners. Newly composed patriotic songs were broadcast along with the calls for mobilization. Every able-bodied man was to report to the draft stations to enlist. "It is every man's patriotic duty to fight the enemy!" In no time and out of nowhere, truckloads of young uniformed men were zooming out of the city, and they were carried to the war front.

My father was thirty-six years old, and he wasn't registered anywhere. Not a single person knew who he was or where he was, and he could have very easily left Kharkov and dissolved into obscurity in the vast country of the Soviet Union. He did not have to enlist, but he did. He was going to fight the Great Patriotic War against Hitler.

After registering for active duty, my father, who changed into the military uniform right there at the registration site, came to say good-bye to my mom and me. He handed over his civilian clothes and told us to sell them and use the money to buy whatever we needed. Then he left. The two of us stayed to fend for ourselves.

When we were in Poland, everyone around me spoke Yiddish so I must not have known much Polish. My mom knew Polish. She was able to pick up a lot of Russian since there are many similarities in the two languages. I learned some Russian from the kids in the apartment building when we all played in the courtyard.

The street corner loudspeakers were continuously dispensing propaganda. Parents were being alerted and strongly advised to take their children to a safe place on the outskirts of the city and to leave them there. "The Communist Party will take good care of the children with food, and they will have priority in evacuation in case such a need should arise."

"Think of your children first, they are our future and our hope. Mothers, do your duty and save your children," a loud strong voice commanded through the loudspeaker.

"We will defeat the enemy! Long live Stalin and his Red Army. Stalin, our father, will lead us to victory."

This information was being blasted day and night, but nobody knew what to expect or how close the front was.

The lines in front of the grocery stores were getting longer. Milk and bread were scarce now. Children no longer played in the streets, and the kiddie land was shut down. The vendors disappeared from the city's streets. No more flowers. No more balloons or suckers. No more ice cream. It was as though none of these things had ever existed. The lines in front of the stores disappeared when the stores were empty. The streetlights were no longer on at night, and every window was masked so that not a flicker of light would betray the city to German bombers. Eventually it was no longer voluntary to send away children into the government compounds.

Now my mom had no choice. With a muffled voice she kept repeating: "It will be better for you. You will be with all the other children. You will have food to eat. There is no more food here. You will be safe."

My mom held my five-and-a-half-year-old hand in hers, squeezing it so hard that it hurt.

I was left on the grounds of a luxurious compound of villas that belonged to the Communist Party elite for their vacations. I never entered the building to which I was assigned. All night long, crying, I held on to the tall, black iron bars of the fence that surrounded the compound. At dawn I saw my mom approaching the gate. Her eyes were also red and swollen.

"Mama, I don't want to be safe, I only want to be with you. I don't care if I starve as long as we do it together."

Both of us weeping hitched a ride on a truck bed back to Kharkov. My mom started to plan our escape from the city. "Are others leaving? Where are they going? Who can we ask? If we leave, will my father know where to find us?"

Suddenly there was no longer time to question or to plan. It was Warsaw all over again. A long wailing of air raid sirens ripped through the air. It was too late to hide even if there was a known place to hide. The bombers were already over our heads. Some people just stood in the streets as the bombs rearranged the city.

Rain fell in sheets that day. My mom hurriedly packed all that we had (not much), and we planted ourselves outside the apartment building, getting soaked and waiting for a miracle. Would anyone show pity and maybe give us a ride to the train station so we could escape again?

A horse-drawn carriage came to a halt in front of us. "Where to?" the man asked.

"Away."

He unloaded us at the train station. He did not accept any money for the ride and wished us good luck. We waited for a train on an open platform. Crowds of people were already there before us.

We waited for days.

A couple of trains zoomed by without as much as slowing down. The one that stopped was already filled to capacity. Some people attempted to squeeze in, but those already inside were pushing back. Even the open caboose was taken, and mobs of soldiers and civilians alike were clamoring for space on the roofs of the train cars.

We ran back and forth alongside the cars, packages dangling from my mom's shoulders and arms, and me holding on to her, scared to loosen my grip. Practically carried by the crowd, my mom and I finally got inside a boxcar of a very long train. People who were already inside were using their bodies to block any available nook where we could possibly place ourselves. We sat squeezed in between a mass of bodies and on top of some bags and suitcases belonging to others. My mom clutched a string-bag with two challas, our only provisions. The teakettle was empty. The water had spilled in the rush for a place in a boxcar.

The two of us were among strangers. My father was in the army on the front lines fighting Hitler. My grandpa was back in occupied Warsaw with Grandma, Aunt Dora, and Uncle Max. Aunt Sara-Rywka was somewhere in the Soviet Union, possibly in Siberia, and Aunt Chajcie was with Estush. We would never know what happened to them.

There were many women with children on the train, and there were some old people who miraculously made it this far. There were also a few young men who were army deserters and some who were running from the draft.

My mom saw one of the young men sneak up in the middle of the night and steal our bread. She may have looked like she was asleep, but she never allowed herself to fully fall asleep, for she needed to watch over me. My mom was so angry. The chutzpah! But she was afraid to confront the bully, for no one knew what some people in some situations might do. It was a hefker velt. The world was up for grabs.

The train rattled along making unpredictable stops and detours. It stopped many times in the middle of nowhere. Every time the train stopped, people would jump out to stretch a little bit and to relieve themselves, if they had not already done so while the train was in motion. Not a single person moved further than arm's length from the train, because one never knew when the train would start moving again. It would usually start without a warning. One had to be able to jump back into the car in a split second. There were rumors of people left behind at such stops and separated from their families forever. Whenever the train would veer or swerve off of its straight course, a wave of panic would spread: "Are we being taken back? Why did they change direction? What's going on?"

Rumors spread fast and easily.

We had no food or water to drink.

We must not have gone too far from the front line when we heard a chilling whistle, a wild howl, a shudder, and then -- boom! A bomb had hit the last two cars of the train and tore them from the rest. Leaving the two graveyard cars behind, the motor-man kept going.

One dark night, through the spaces between the boards of the boxcar's walls, someone spotted lights twinkling in the distance. A settlement that we had just passed did not need to black out their windows. This was a good sign, synonymous with peace. Of course, the people in the village couldn't have known that only a few short hours from their homes our train had been bombed and that the war was coming close.

I did not ask for food or drink. I knew that my mom did not have any to give. What was the use of asking or crying? Another unscheduled stop was made. We saw smoke rising from chimneys. It was a sign of a populated settlement. The settlement seemed so close even though the houses looked awfully small. Without saying a word, my mom grabbed the empty kettle and sprung toward the village. I saw her run and run. A long while passed and I wished that my mom was already back.

A jerk, a huff, a pss . . . and a burst of white steam enveloped the entire train. With another jerk and a squeak of the wheels the train began to move. Partially burned-out coal produced cinders that flew all around and got into the wagons through every opening. The train picked up speed. I cried for my mama. No one, not a single person, looked at me. Sitting on top of all our worldly possessions in the hot, foul-smelling place with wall-to-wall people, I didn't care about water or food, but how would I know when to get off the train or where to go? Who would help me find my mom?

Between stops, the train seemed to be moving much longer than ever before. The village into which my mom had disappeared was gone from sight a long, long time ago. I didn't know the name of the village. It may not even have had a name. I wouldn't even know which direction the train was going since it was constantly changing tracks, once going east, then going south, then a little bit north, and then south again, deeper into the Soviet Union.

Finally the train stopped. It made no difference to me. I wasn't making any decisions. I didn't even have to go to relieve myself since had not had any food or drink for days. Someone slid the door open to let some fresh air in and let some of the stench out. I didn't pay attention to anything until I noticed a bloody and disheveled body clutching a familiar looking teakettle. She crawled into the wagon. Without a sound, my mom hugged me. The kettle, which she was unable to release from her grip, was hurting my back. I didn't mind.

My mom had found a well in the small, isolated farming town, and she filled the kettle with water to bring back to the train. On her way back she saw that the train was chugging away. She began to run to catch up with it, and she finally managed to jump onto some fragments sticking out of the debris left after the bomb shore off the two last cars of the train.

As bad as the conditions on the train were, they began to get even worse. People were becoming meaner and louder and more vulgar. The stench was unbearable. Everyone had lice. Not a soul had water or food. The only consolation was that, with every hour, we were further and further away from the war zone.

1936, Fela with father and a group of neighborhood kids, likely in Nowy-Dwo'r on summer vacation.

No one, not a single person, looked at me.

AFTER LEAVING KHARKOV | FELA DOGADKO

Another horrible day on the train. Then, unexplained stop, one of many. My mom woke me and showed me, through a crack in the door, flickering lights in the far distance. Lights were always a reason for elation and for hope.

Noiselessly my mom tied the bundles of all our worldly possessions together and eased them out the door. Then she jumped out and motioned to me to jump into her outstretched arms.

Fela's mother, Anna, pre-war.

Some of our belongings consisted of a featherbed, a pillow, and two sheets, which were squeezed into a sack. A second bag held some clothes and my father's suit, which he left for us to sell after he enlisted in the army. We also had the treasure of a silver place-setting service that my mom swore she didn't pack when we left Warsaw. She suspected that her mother, my grandma, had put it there in secret. The silver was a wedding present when Anna Kellerwajs married Zelik Hershfang in 1929.

My mom carried the bundles swinging from her neck and across her body. In her hands she held the teakettle and a knapsack with photos and letters. Even so, she offered to carry me in her arms after a short rest on the moist ground. I hadn't had a chance to stretch my legs in the many, many days on the train. I wore my coat, which was still encased in the burlap cover that Pesa had made for it in Bialystok.

The air smelled so good. Soon I could also see some lights inside the houses with unshaded windows. From the train, the lights of the settlement seemed so close, but the closer we got, the further the lights seemed to move away. We walked and we walked.

One by one the lights in the settlement were going out and we were soon in total darkness. We "camped" out in a field and waited for daybreak. I was shivering inside my very warm coat and it was still summer, but I remembered what my mom always said, that things would look better in the morning. They always do.

At first light we were able to make out human voices coming from the village. A kind Russian family took us in and gave us a place to sleep. There was plenty of water from a well. My hair was washed with homemade brown soap then kerosene rubbed in, and the lice and their eggs, little by little, came out with a fine-tooth comb. The process was repeated daily for weeks. I smelled like the wick of a filled kerosene lamp for a long, long time. But the lice were gone and my hair was nice and shiny, and I stopped scratching.

With the men on the front, the women did all the farm work. By early fall every person was at work in a grain elevator. My mom raked the grain, and I liked to jump or just lie on top of the warm stacks of grain. I was never more than a few steps away from her.

Individually, the members of the collective farm grew pumpkins in their very small plots of land. They baked the pumpkins in large Russian ovens until they got to be fragrant and sweet as honey. At first, although I was really hungry, the unfamiliar food didn't taste good to me. But in time, with no choice, I started to like it. Sometimes the family got some milk and "baked" the milk. A clay pot full of milk would sit in the oven for hours. When it came out of the oven it was covered with a thick, delicious brown crust. Sometimes, I put a piece of it on top of a slice of pumpkin, and it tasted like heaven.

Like in Kharkov, we could have waited out the war here, but it wasn't to be. The air began to smell like gunpowder and fire again. Recent memories of the sounds of German bombers came back. The people of the village were on edge. They were wary of the strangers among them, especially the Jews. My mom and I had to leave.

We went mostly by train. At times we traveled by horse-drawn wagons full of hay, or, on occasion, by truck. We passed cities large and small. Some of the cities' names I still remember, some I have long since forgotten, some may not even have had names. Woronez, Engels, Volgograd, Astrakhan. In Astrakhan, a city that lay on the delta of the Volga River where it meets the Caspian Sea, the train stopped. As soon as the train stopped, the passengers frantically gathered any available containers and sprinted toward the beach. The shore was covered with globs of salt. The salt was dark gray and it had sand mixed in, but miles from there even this impure salt was worth its weight in gold, and somehow people knew that. I don't know by what design or what chance we kept on inching toward the Soviet Republic of Uzbekistan.

We eventually came to Tashkent and settled in a collective farm about fifteen kilometers outside the capital. We lived there until the end of the war.

Before we got to Collective Farm No. 15, we passed many beautiful and exotic places in the Fergana Valley. The collective was surrounded by mountains covered with blooming blood-red poppies. We stayed there with Uzbeki nomads. The population was sparse in the region. Nomadic animal herding was still the prevalent way of life. Their land was semiarid. There were about ten inches of rainfall each year, but the people had devised an elaborate system of irrigation, aryki, which helped them to grow grass on which goats and sheep could graze. Still, the shepherds had to move their herds from place to place. Although the Soviet government nationalized everything, the Uzbeks still managed to own some of their land, houses, animals, gardens with fruit trees, and the poppy fields. The shepherds shepherded the animals while riding beautiful horses. They wore long sheepskin coats and karakul hats that made them look very rich.

We were not at all familiar with the geological history of this part of the planet. One night the earth shook. We thought that we were being bombed and that we would be buried alive or burned. It turned out to be an earthquake, which was, in many ways, a relief. The earthquake sounded like collapsing buildings whose weight made the earth tremble, and like derailed trains folding like accordions.

Wide cracks, through which we could see the outside, appeared in our one-room mud hut, and a long crevice divided a large area of land outside. The earth continued to vibrate and shake as if it was trying to shake us off its back.

The nomads were suddenly separated by the divide. Many of their yurtas remained on one side, and the other bunch of skin tents ended up on the other side. The nomads cut down a few large trees and laid them across the ravine to make a bridge. Horsemen, however, did not need the bridge. Their horses could jump across. Many animals fell to their deaths into the depth of the ravine during the earthquake, and many more sheep and goats fell trying to jump across the crevice.

The day after the earthquake, a horseman, clad in all of his fineries, came to us with offerings of food. Since the Uzbeks speak their own distinct language (Russian was taught in schools but not accepted at home), my mom could not understand what the Uzbek was saying while he presented us with the food. Everything became clear when a second Russian-speaking representative of the wealthy landowner appeared the following day.

The wealthy landowner wanted my mom to be his second wife. He was a young man, just establishing his harem. My mom must have either pretended not to understand him or was too startled to say anything. Then another man came with a revised offer. My mom, by being older than his first wife, would be considered wife number one, and of course she could bring her kazymka, meaning me, with her. My mom frantically packed our belongings and again we ran. I would never know what life in a harem was like.

By the time I was six years old, I'd already had over two years of war experience. I had been away from home a long time. Uzbekistan was, to me, the end of the world. It was a strangely peaceful place. But what if Hitler's airplanes followed us to these beautiful blue and sunny skies? From this place there would be nowhere else to run.

For almost the next four years, our home was a single room in a row of poorly built, sand-toned rooms of mud and straw which were put together in a hurry. The dirt floor smelled of dung. There were no windows. Two small berths of rough wooden planks, one on top of the other, took up practically the entire space of the room. Daylight was trickling in through a poorly fitted door. When we were out my mom would tie a piece of rope around the hook on the wall to a hook on the door to keep the door closed, and I would inadvertently ask, "Why bother to tie the door when it could be so easily untied by just anybody?" And my mom would always answer: "No lock in the hands of a thief is safe. This piece of rope is protecting the entrance to our room from honest people." Our puny room was dreadfully bleak, gloomy, and so blissfully quiet. The whistling of falling bombs and the frightful shrieks of air raid sirens were left behind us. A small plot of land separated the row of rooms from a huge cemetery. The fence around the cemetery was crooked and it was falling apart. The few remaining boards of the fence looked like skeletons at night, and in the day they spread scary shadows, but we weren't at all scared to play in or around the cemetery. We knew who was causing the terrible problems in the world, and it wasn't dead people.

Daily, a group of old Uzbek men from a nearby village would congregate by the wayside, lean against a tall fence which surrounded the apple orchard, and smoke their water pipes. The pipes made quiet gurgling noises whenever the men puffed. These complaisant men must have told each other everything they had to say a long, long time ago. Now they stood strung out like crows on a wire. They seemed content in just being.

During the day, even the air was too lazy to move. In spite of the stifling heat, the Uzbeks wore their quilted jackets, explaining that the jackets protected them from the heat and mosquitoes. In the peace and quiet we could hear growling stomachs, my mother's weeping, hyenas and packs of jackals, and the whine of bloodthirsty mosquitoes.

I was always hungry. I couldn't believe it when my mother told me that I refused to eat a banana when I was a little girl in Warsaw. What did a banana taste like? What did it smell like? Only two years had gone by, and I couldn't remember what it felt like not to go to bed hungry.

Then, in the winter, the barracks in which we lived were not unlike the ones in Uzbekistan, except that they were built of wood and the doors opened into the arctic winds of the outside. My five-year-old neighbor's babushka kept busy all day long inside their one room. A large Russian oven occupied a prominent place in the room. In the fall, the grandma sealed the window with wads of cotton wool. She sealed every littlest crack with great precision. She mindfully checked the seal with a lit candle which she guided slowly along the perimeter of the window. When the candle flame fluttered, she would squeeze more cotton into the cracks until the flame of the candle held still and upright.

Only then was she satisfied with her job that the window was tucked in for the winter, not to be opened before late into the spring.

Tucking in the door took the labor of Sisyphus. The cold wind, rain, and snow easily entered the room through large gaps between the door and its frame. The grandma used an inverted pail to reach the top of the door and she tried to fill every opening with cotton wool. Thanks to her efforts, their room, unlike mine next door, was snug and cozy even when the wind howled outside and it was freezing.

My mom worked long days. I was too young to keep a fire going, even if I had wood and coal, and I had no grandma. So, invited or not, I spent the time after daycare with my friend and his grandma next door until my mom came home. I often opened the door to check whether my mom was back or not. Every time I opened the door the pieces of cotton flew out of every previously sealed spot. The babushka must have liked me a whole lot. She was never angry with me for opening and closing the door so frequently.

The family used the big oven primarily for keeping the room warm. Like us, they didn't have much food to cook. They got their few daily pieces of coal by following a coal delivery wagon and picking up the coal that would sometimes fall into the street. They saved every bit of the few corn plants that grew under the window. The dried stalks, leaves, and rare pieces of newspaper, made good fire starter. All of this, and the stove made cheerful crackling sounds. On top of the large stove a pot looked very lonely, but filled with water it produced happy bubbling sounds, and the billowy clouds of steam escaped into the air like food being cooked. All I needed was some imagination to fill in the smells and tastes.

Sometimes, for a very special treat, the grandma would put a handful of dried kernels of corn on top of the stove when it was very hot. The kernels soon started to explode and take off all the way to the ceiling. My friend and I would run around the room catching as many of the flying popped corn kernels as we could. I do not remember this Russian babushka's name nor the name of the town she was from, but I know, for sure, that she was the one who invented popcorn!

In Keebray, my mom and I shared one bowl of soup a day. According to the Communist doctrine, one who does not work does not eat. I did not work. With one small bowl of watered down soup between us, my mom was just pretending to eat, pushing the soup my way. While others grumbled about the watered down soup, my mom always said that at least here we did not have bombs falling on our heads, and we could see the clear blue sky and enjoy the sunshine. She would tell of a fond memory of her grandma and chicken soup.

Every Friday, my great grandma made soup for the entire family. She could never afford to buy more than one chicken and she didn't want to "weaken" the broth by adding too much water, so after dividing the broth there was never any left for her. She then, supposedly hiding the fact from others, would add to her noodles the water in which the noodles were boiled.

This was the same great grandma I remember for bringing candy every time she came to see me. She would never just hand the candy over to me. She would put it inside the pocket of one of her numerous petticoats. She wore just as many aprons over the petticoats. It became a fun routine, a game, because I had to guess in which petticoat the candy was hidden. When I found it, probably after many tries, she kvelled, she clapped her hands and told everybody how smart I was.

My mom didn't let on, but I figured out that our entire family in Warsaw had been wiped out. I began to see my grandfather's face everywhere. I saw him in the face of Lenin, on pedestals, on murals, on plaques, and everywhere imaginable.

They both had the same kind of goatee and the same kind of hairline. Why couldn't my grandpa have escaped with us? Why did he have to return to Warsaw? I missed all of my family, but I think I missed them because my mom missed them. I really didn't remember any of them anymore, except my grandpa.

Grandfather Baruch Kellerwajs was gentle and admired his only grandchild by his first-born daughter so very much. He always used to kiss every finger on my hand and every toe on my feet, ever so gently and delicately and with such delight. Before my grandfather said his final good-byes at the Neutral Zone, he kissed my fingers, and when he got to kiss my pinky, he took me aside and whispered in my ear, "Just between the two of us, the little freckle on your pinky is not really a freckle. After so many kisses a hair of my red beard has become stuck there forever and ever. Now, whenever you look at your pinky, what everyone else thinks is a freckle, you'll be the only one to know that it's not. It is a part of me with love to you, for you to remember me by." Wiping my wet cheek, I believed him.

When I was a little girl and looked at the freckle on my pinky, I giggled. Now when I look at the freckle, I shed a tear.

I remember the Tashkent's open-air shuk, where merchants spread their wares on the ground. Some of the merchants had an enormous number of beautiful silk rugs to sell, others had only a few dried apricots or raisins laid out on the top of a cloth in front of them. Some sold lepyoshkas (pita bread) and their smell made me drool. The market was crowded, noisy, dusty, and a lot of fun.

I was not at all interested in the magnificent rugs, the magically colorful silk and cotton textiles, furs, gemstones, or exotic aromatic spices. My focus was the pita, the dried fruits, and the almonds. I couldn't think of anything but food. Hunger has that effect on people.

"Kazymka, Kazymka, come and sample my apricots."

"Taste mine and tell me if they are not the sweetest in the entire market."

"My raisins are so plump, you could taste the juice in them, taste a couple and tell me if I am not right."

A taste of some prune from one vendor, an apricot from another, a couple of nuts from yet another, and my six-year-old stomach was full. I even succeeded in saving a few pieces of food for my mom, carefully placed in my pocket.

I wandered around the shuk, and all the while I kept an eye on my mom, for I feared separation from her much more than I feared hunger.

The Uzbeks were the most hospitable people anywhere. Whenever the two of us passed an Uzbek family's dwelling, they would invite us in. If it just so happened that they were about to sit down for a meal, we were asked to join them and share.

The meal was a wonderful rice dish with almonds, raisins, spices, and sometimes chunks of lamb. Our expeditions into the neighborhood were intentional. Familiar with their custom of great hospitality, my mom would follow her nose into dinnertime, and she would gratefully accept the generosity.

Malaria.

I didn't want my mom to give me most of her soup. I was afraid that she would get weak from hunger and maybe not survive the next malaria attack. Then what? What would happen to me? I did not even know how to read yet.

My mom kept me in preschool beyond my first grade age because in preschool I was given a snack every day. The snack was always kisiel (thin gelatin). It looked like slime and I could tell that it was sweetened with saccharin because of the bitter aftertaste. I hated it.

We had been living on the collective farm for over a year now. I liked it there a lot. The sun was bright and warm. But I did not like having malaria and I cried sometimes. I hid my tears because they made my mom very sad. I didn't want to upset her more than she already was. She also suffered from malaria, and I never knew what to do for her.

The mosquitoes were the middlemen of malaria. They swarmed over the feces-polluted water in the nearby slow-moving creek. This is where we got our drinking water.

Malaria attacks came with clockwork regularity, every seventy-two hours. I would first get the chills for longer than an hour. My mom wrapped me like a mummy in the same feather bed we had carried from our home in Warsaw. It would slip out from under me because I trembled and shook. I could not stop my shivering or my teeth from chattering, even though the temperature outside was 105 degrees or higher. The chills had to run their course no matter what. After the chills, the fever would attack. The fever stage would go on for some four hours, at least, sometimes going up to 104 degrees. Then the fever broke and the sweats came. Even my long, thick hair dripped wet, and I felt thirsty. I took quinine, when available. The whites of my eyes were yellow and my skin had a yellowish tinge. I was still weak and aching from an attack when I felt the next one coming on. For over three years malaria was a part of my life.

I couldn't **think** of anything but **food.**

Fela, seven years old; taken in Uzbekistan

HIDING IN THE OPEN | PETER GERSHANOV

In early 1939, my father, who was a very successful winemaker in Trnava, Czechoslovakia, decided that

to stay in the country was too dangerous. He saw that there was a war coming, and he felt that Jews were going to be persecuted. He was, of course, right on both counts. Leaving my mother, brother and me in our hometown, he arranged to go to Great Britain by having an English customer send him a letter of complaint regarding the quality of a shipment of wine he had just received. The wine was "sour" and it needed his personal attention.

Post-war — small farm where Peter hid with his mother and brother near Bresova, Slovakia.

REFLECTION : HOLLY GERSHANOV NELSON (Daughter of Peter Gershanov)

Indeed, Trnava had a vibrant community of nearly 2,500 Jews in 1939; it was reduced to 150 Survivors after the war, with none living there today. The main sanctuary of my dad's synagogue was stripped of its pews to become a Nazi horse stable during the war. In 1945, my dad, uncle, and grandmother davened with 18 Survivors in a small school room adjacent to the sanctuary in their synagogue.

Today, the synagogue building is the home of temporary modern art exhibits. There is no bimah. No ark. No Torah. The former synagogue, like the town of Trnava, stands as a living memory of a Jewish community that is merely a repository of the fading recollections of a few Survivors.

On his way from Czechoslovakia, he stopped in Prague on March 15, 1939, the day the Germans took over the city. He managed to get out and arrived in London a week later. When he arrived there he sought and received refugee status. This enabled him to ask for permission to send for us. It was not granted.

When the Battle of Britain started, he contacted his cousins in Chicago, who sponsored his immigration to the United States. He managed to immigrate immediately and started the process for our family to follow him. Mother, Fred, and I received appointments at the United States embassy in Budapest, Hungary in November 1941. We were there, waiting in our hotel on December 7, 1941 when the attack on Pearl Harbor took place. The United States declared war on Germany and its allies and the United States embassy closed immediately. We returned to Trnava. At that time my brother was six, and I was nine. The way back to Trnava was one of the few times that I can remember my mother showing any signs of fear or emotional distress. Little did we know that it would be five years before we were reunited with my father.

The three of us, my grandmother and my Uncle Poldi remained in Trnava. We were not deported, thanks to the help of my father's ex-employees, from the "Arizator" (the Aryan who was chosen to take over my father's business), some fake documents that Uncle Poldi had printed up, some money that we had hidden, and a lot of luck. My mother, who was twenty-seven in 1939, showed astounding resiliency, fortitude, and nerve.

My grandmother survived the war hidden in the basement of the home of one of my fathers ex-employees. Unfortunately my uncle's luck ran out. While saying good-bye to friends as they were loaded into railroad cars, he was included in the transport. He did not survive the camps, and neither did my other uncle and his wife.

Because I was blond and blue-eyed, I was sometimes sent with messages into the jail, where some of the Jewish men were held while awaiting transport. Sometimes they waited there for months. My luck held. The only memory I have of those errands is the overwhelming stench of urine.

In July 1944 the situation in Trnava became untenable. The man who was hiding my grandmother arranged for us to move to a tiny farm in the lower western Carpathian mountains of Slovakia. My mother, brother and I hid from the Slovak Nazi's there until April 1945. There is a picture, taken some time after the war, of our hosts Stefan Markos, and his wife Suzannah, and their children Olga, Anna, and Jan. The farm owner, Stefan had lost an arm in a threshing accident. He was not able to work his farm efficiently. The money we paid him made the difference for his and his wife's survival, so they staked their lives on hiding us.

Their small farm was in a small settlement of houses that were about one kilometer apart, near a village named Brezova Pod Bradlo (Brezova under the Bradlo). Bradlo is the tomb of the Slovak World War I hero Rastislav Stefanik, who with Tomas Masarik and Edvard Benesh, helped to established Czechoslovakia in 1918. Stafanik was killed in a plane crash in 1919, and the other two became the successive presidents of Czechoslovakia. The monument is on top of a mountain that is completely surrounded by a ring of somewhat smaller mountains.

I climbed to the top of the monument often, as there was not much to do on the small farm. One day in late August 1944, I was lying on my back, looking up at the sky when I heard a slight buzzing sound. The noise became that of airplanes, kept getting louder and louder. Soon planes dotted the sky from horizon to horizon. The noise was so loud, amplified by the ring of surrounding mountains, that it absolutely terrified me. I do not remember even leaving the top of the mountain, but the next thing I knew, I was at the bottom. I was also terrified by the rain of brass shell casings that fell around me. The bomber crews were cleaning up their plane floors of spent ammunition. Much later I found out that the American planes were on the final mission to finish the destruction of the oil fields at Ploesti, Romania. The Germans were very dependent on the oil from these fields, and its unavailability was another nail in the German coffin.

Sometime later in September we heard the sound of a low flying plane with its engines sputtering. This was followed by a loud crash that seemed to be extremely close. Without asking my mother, just telling my brother, I joined a small group of farm boys who were walking toward the crash site. Fortunately they were not in the least interested in why a city boy like me was living in their primitive farm environment. We started on what we thought would be a short trip, but did not arrive at the site for at least two hours.

The American plane's fuselage was split in half lengthwise. There were at least six unexploded bombs lying around, as well as large quantities of aluminum chaff (thrown out of planes to confuse radar). People used the chaff for decorating Christmas trees because it resembled tinsel. I do not remember any intact bodies, but there was completely bare leg cut off below the knee. Possibly the rest of the crew had parachuted out.

Fortunately, the Slovak authorities did not arrive while our little group was at the scene. We took a large quantity of chaff and also some fifty caliber ammunition. (The bullets were half an inch in diameter and seven inches long.) They exploded wonderfully when stuck in the side of a mud cartwheel rut with a small fire built under them. We had enough sense to move a safe distance away after lighting the fire. This provided us with a great amount of fun.

Later that same night we heard four loud explosions coming from the direction of the crash. We never knew if the bombs had exploded or were set off by someone. The explosions were much louder than our own ammunition explosions.

Well into the fall of 1944, we heard that partisans had come through our little settlement at night. We didn't see or hear them. There were occasional German patrols, which never came close to us. They kept mostly to the ridgelines. One morning we found out that an "elderly" couple (in their fifties), living about one kilometer from us, had both been shot in the head by partisans. The partisans thought that they had cooperated with a German patrol that had stopped close to their house the previous day.

The snow started to fall in November, and by the beginning of December everything was covered by about three feet of snow, including the dirt roads. One day, early in December, the farmer's daughter Olga and I went into the barn that was attached to the house. As usual, we were playing with a hand-operated machine that cut hay into small pieces, enabling the cow to eat and digest it more easily. As Olga turned the crank, I put my right index finger on the gears as they moved under it. Suddenly my finger got caught between the gears and got crushed almost to the second knuckle. This accident could have cost us our lives.

My mother convinced our fearful, hesitant host, Stefan, to take us to Brezova. My mother, Stefan, and I got into a sleigh pulled by a horse, which Stefan managed to borrow. My brother, who was eight at that time, was left behind so that if we were caught, at least he had a chance of survival. It was the first time in his life that he had been left alone. My mother, who was extremely strong in almost every other aspect, could not deal with my mangled hand, so I tied a tourniquet around my own wrist before we left.

We arrived in town after dark and went to the town's only doctor. I think he knew instantly that we were Jews but did not ask any questions as he started to work on my finger. I did not know, at the age of twelve, to loosen the tourniquet occasionally. My hand had lost all of its feeling by that time. The doctor shot the finger with local anesthetic and cleaned it. He cut and sutured to save as much of my finger as he could. He required assistance, but Mother, who had so calm and strong since the war started, was unable to assist him. I managed to hand him the instruments that he required with my left hand. The pale bloody hand that was sticking out of a white sheet between us did not seem to be attached to me. The procedure took no more that forty-five minutes; to my mother it must have seemed an eternity. He only had a sulfa power as a disinfectant, which he put on my finger before sending us on our way.

We made our way back to the farm without incident. Later that night after the local anesthetic wore off, the pain in my finger was excruciating. We did not even have an aspirin to relive it. That night was the only time in my life that I considered suicide as a way to escape the pain. The pain went away after a few days. I was extremely lucky not to get an infection. (After the war and our immigration to the United States, my mother sent the doctor, whose name I do not remember, many "care" packages. They were in gratitude for his help for not reporting us as Jews and risking his own life in the process.)

We managed to go through the rest of the winter without any further incidents. In March our hosts started to get increasingly nervous. They heard rumors of Russian advances and German resistance. In early April we were asked to leave. Mother could not get them to change their minds. It's possible that by that time we had run out of money. We packed up our suitcases and Stefan drove us to the train station in Brezova. The train soon arrived and we boarded it. We were three Jews without papers and even without train tickets. Our luck continued because our section of Slovakia was in total panic. People were fleeing in all directions, toward the Russians, away from the Russians. It was a wonder the train was still running at all.

We arrived in Trnava without getting challenged by anyone and walked about a mile to the house where my grandmother was hidden. I walked far ahead of my mother and brother in case were challenged. Grandmother's host agreed to put us up. We all knew that it would be for a short time only. It was a week later that the Russians arrived in Trnava, and we were lucky again. The Germans at that time made a stand every forty to fifty miles. They fought the Russians for a short time and then fell back to the west. They made a stand east of Trnava and fell back west of it, sparing us.

As I look back at those war years, and the day-to-day uncertainty of survival, I do not recall great fear. I credit my mother with keeping us alive, and sheltering us from the reality of the dangers we faced, in spite of my preteen rebellious behavior.

RED ARMY | PETER GERSHANOV

In the spring of 1945, my mother, nine year-old brother, and I (twelve) left our hiding place near Brezova, Czechoslovakia, in the lower Carpathian Mountains.

We had spent about a year there, living in one tiny room. We could no longer stay because our hosts decided that it was too dangerous for them if we remained. The retreating Germans might come through the area. Rumors spread that the Russians were advancing to the west against German resistance.

Our host, John Markov, drove us to the Brezova railroad station. We boarded a train going southwest for the fifty-mile trip to Trnava, our hometown. We had nothing, no train tickets, no documents, and not much money. The train was half full with other refugees who were trying to get away from the oncoming Russians. No conductor was in sight, no police, no Gestapo, no one to check anything. We were able to get off the train in Trnava without incident.

We walked, each carrying a suitcase, to the home of one of my father's employees. He had arranged our hiding place in the mountains and hid our grandmother after we had left. With the panic induced by the oncoming Russians, no one paid any attention to three more refugees walking on the street.

Our new host did not seem too surprised to see us. He ushered us to a small basement room, which was about ten by twelve feet. My grandmother hid there whenever someone was visiting. After a joyful reunion, we settled in. We had no idea how long we would be there, but we knew, from the rumors and the number of refugees our host had seen, that it would be for a short time only. I recall an outhouse behind the house. It had been shot up and was full of bullet holes. There probably was indoor plumbing as well.

Within a few days we heard the faint sound of large guns. About two days later we heard the screech of rockets followed by loud explosions. Later we found out that Russian Katyushas (rockets) had destroyed Trnava's railroad station. How lucky we were again to have arrived at the station just a few days earlier. After hearing the noise of the rocket attack, our hosts did not go out of the house again.

The Germans' way of fighting in our area was to fall back from the advancing Russians about thirty to forty miles, dig in, fight, and then fall back again. Luckily for us, Trnava lay in the center of such a fallback zone. The fighting occurred fifteen miles east of us, and then again fifteen miles west of us. Trnava was spared. The only damage to the town was the destruction of the rocketed railroad station.

As the Russians came closer, all of us, including our hosts, crammed into the small basement room. We were not on a main road, and we did not hear very much from the outside. After a few hours of silence, my brother and I dared to venture upstairs. From the front window, we saw a group of Russian soldiers on horseback. We immediately ran back downstairs. Not too long after this we heard the noise above of the Russian fighters entering our house. Then we heard them descend the stairs.

Four Red Army soldiers with guns came down. The biggest Russian had the largest gun I had ever seen. It was so long that he could not stand it upright in a room with an eight-foot ceiling. Later I found out that it was an anti-tank gun.

As soon as they came down they started harassing us to give them our watches. One of the soldiers pulled up his uniform sleeve, so we could see that he had watches from his wrist to his elbow. The soldiers were not very belligerent, but none of us could take our eyes off their guns. Before we could comply with their orders, we were saved by the arrival of their lieutenant. He ordered all of them upstairs. With the lieutenant protecting us, we all followed him upstairs.

After talking to the lieutenant, we found out that he was Jewish. He explained to us that the Soviets had emptied their jails of criminal prisoners (not political ones), and that they had been assigned to the front lines where they faced the greatest dangers. They had been the ones who first came down into the basement.

Later, my brother and I visited the lieutenant at his encampment. There we sat around a campfire, drinking tea and eating sweets for the first time in five years, and learning Russian songs. Without prompting, the two of us, naive as we were, swore eternal allegiance to the Red Army, our saviors.

A few days after our liberation we gathered at our synagogue. Our Hebrew school teacher, a Survivor, managed to contact all of the Survivors who had returned to Trnava. The main sanctuary had no pews, and had been used as a horse stable by the Nazis. But as there were only about eighteen of us, we easily fit into one of the least damaged schoolrooms. I remember everyone crying and hugging, even though most of us did not know each other. After everyone calmed down somewhat, the teacher conducted services.

Before the Kaddish, a few people tried to say the names of their murdered relatives, but they soon broke down and gave up. This was, without a doubt, the most moving experience of my life.

Eventually, about 150 Jewish Survivors returned to Trnava. In 1939, the Jewish population had been 2,000 to 2,500 Jews.

RECOLLECTING MY LIFE | JOE KOENIG

You had to fight to survive the Holocaust.

Nobody survived by chance. You had to survive by any means. You had to use your brain. You had to use every bit of knowledge you had. You had to work at it with every ounce of energy you possessed.

Every Survivor has a different story to tell. A completely different story. What worked for one didn't work for the next. The will to survive was enormous. If you had the will, you would do anything to survive. Still, sometimes it didn't work. Some people tried to survive with all of their might and were eliminated. That happened a lot. If someone caught on that you were a Jew, even just part Jewish, you could be turned in.

Now, when I look back, I wonder how all of this happened, and I wonder how I survived. It took guts, perseverance, and a certain kind of genius to survive the Holocaust. It took a lot to go through it all and still come out a decent person. There had to be a lot of decency in you before the Nazis came. At your school, in your parents, an upbringing that gave you patience, wisdom, and knowledge of how to act in life. There were people who became animals and lost their decency. Maybe they had to do that in order to survive. If you had to act like an animal in order to survive, you did it. Wanting to preserve your life can make you act like an animal if you have to.

Joe Koenig at 26 years old, US Army 1953.

Sarah, Joe and Theodore Koenig.

'If you had to act like an animal in order to survive, you did it.'

THE BALCONY OFF KASZTELANSKA STREET | JANINE OBERROTMAN

Under sunlit sky
I sit
On my balcony
And think of death.

It must be Sunday.
Empty is the street below.
Across, from an open window,
A sound rises.

It resonates, it grows,
It fills the street
With loud, persistent, unavoidable sound.
It fills the air crannies with a lover's lament:

"...He called her a sweet name of Charmee,
Charmee, Charmee,
And she was his sunshine . . . "

The sound rises and falls
Before it ends,
It starts again:
"Charmee, Charmee, Charmee . . ."

Last night the kitten died.
For us, death too will come.
How warm is the sun on my face,
How sweet it feels . . .

It is a dirge I should sing!
A farewell lament to sun,
To home,
To life!

Last Friday
No candles were lit.
No candles will ever be lit again
By my mother
In the house on Kasztelanska Street.

Tomorrow is roundup time:
Tomorrow we may die
Violent deaths.

The world will go on,
Sun will rise and warm people's faces,
And they will play Charmee
On the old record player:

" . . . And he called her a sweet name of
Charmee,
And she was his sunshine . . ."

Janine, 1945.

REFLECTION : JANINE OBERROTMAN

You think you could never have lived without your mother. Someday, you will. Your life was tragic because of loss and happy because you overcame. You will have a good life, three sons! What more could you wish for?

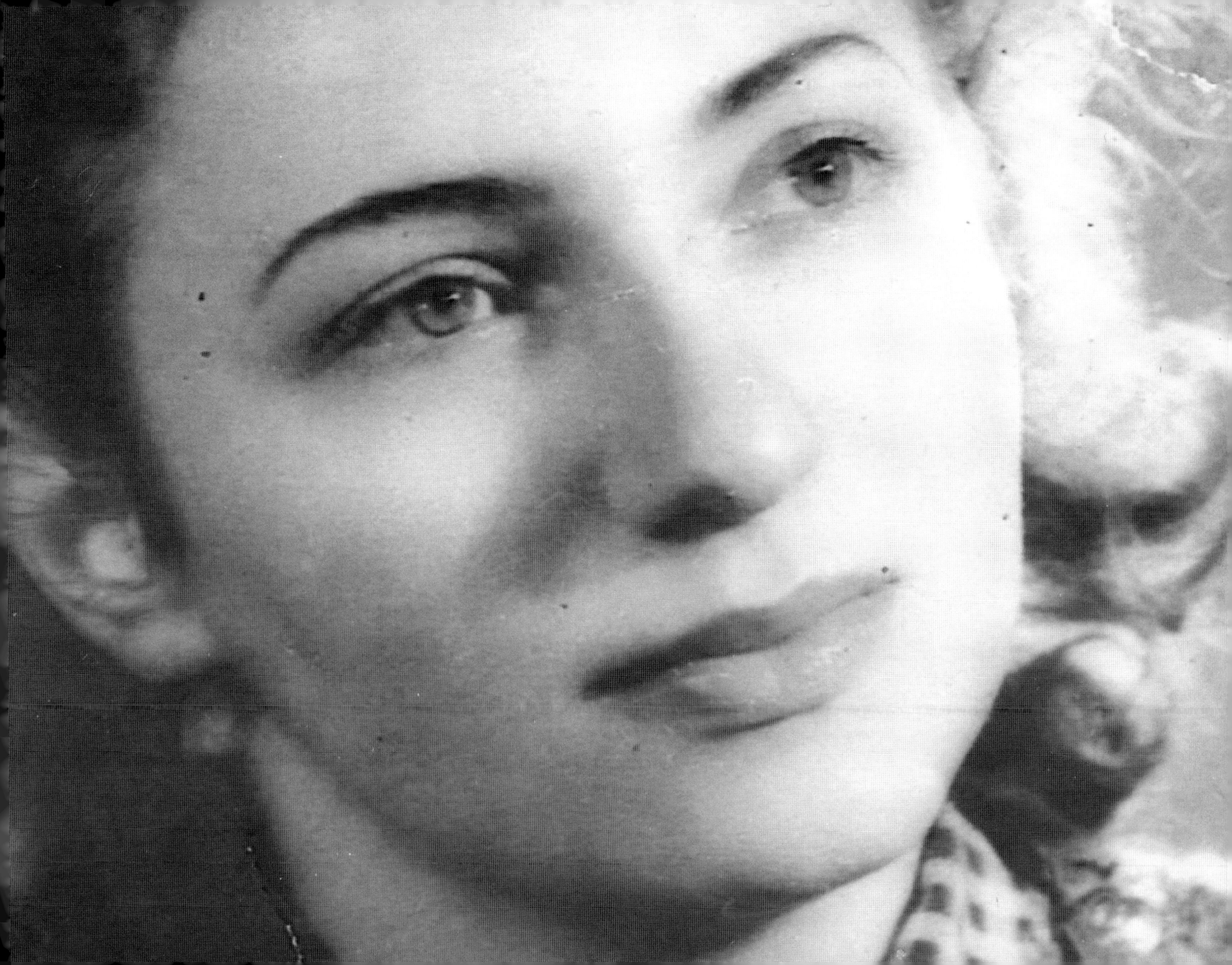

THE TEACHER | JANINE OBERROTMAN

I can still hear

the sound of their steps

on the cobblestones of Grodecka Street. It reverberates, even now, in my ears. A long, gray-blue column stretches forth, seemingly without end. They march with the goose step of conquerors. It is June 29, 1941, eleven o'clock in the morning, and the victorious German army is now entering Lvov. The Russians have fled.

Janine and her mother "Moushka" in 1936.

I stand alone on the balcony of the side street building and watch. I realize, in my inexperienced fifteen-year-old soul, that my life, as it was lived until now, is over. It will never be the same.

But this story is not supposed to be about me. It is about my teacher. For three months she makes me forget who and where I am. I have months of freedom in a time of persecution.

My parents put me under house arrest. In the city there are pogroms, there are roundups and random killings. Everyone over fourteen years of age has to wear a white armband with a blue Star of David. The armband has designated dimensions. Some people put it under plastic to make it last longer. This band will isolate us further from other ethnic groups; unlike the others, we are to become a visible target.

My parents and I live in a mixed neighborhood that is relatively quiet. The Jews here represent a very small minority. Even so, I have to stay home. Father goes to work on construction. Mother tries to feed us by bartering our linens and other possessions with peasants who come to the door. I study. In the beginning, I study from the textbooks I have leftover from previous school years. Soon my supply runs out. I do not want to study math or science, only the comfort subjects like foreign languages, especially French and German, history, and literature. I yield more to my ambitions than to my fears. I want to feel like a normal person, especially since I cannot live like one. Under German occupation, education is forbidden to Jews, both students and teachers, under penalty of death.

I have a short reprieve when I discover pages from a history book left to use as toilet paper in a bathroom we share with our neighbors. Usually the newspaper, properly cut, serves this purpose. Now, to my total surprise, instead of reading the outdated news in the washroom, I have the detailed description of the battle of Zama, when Hannibal, the Carthaginian general in the Second Punic War, was decisively defeated by the Romans in 202 BCE.

I promise my neighbors that from now on I will be responsible for the paper in the washroom. It will come from my father's supply of old Jewish newspapers. As a consequence, I come into possession of twenty volumes of illustrated world history, a beautifully illustrated tome of complete plays by Schiller and some other books whose titles now escape me.

I keep on reading them and when I finish, I start rereading them by the sunny window in my parents' bedroom. My mother sits on one of the beds. My father may be there also. We have to gather in one room as only one can be heated.

I have just discovered that I have no more French books from which to study. I turn to mother and say angrily, "How in the world will I be able to go to university if I can't go to school?" My mother doesn't say anything but looks at me as if I am out of my mind. I realize immediately why she does so, and I am sorry. It is totally unrealistic and foolish to come out with such a ridiculous outburst. I understand this in the bottom of my empty stomach, and the fear that has lived in every fiber of my body, the fear that I have tried so hard to bury since the day on the balcony when I saw and heard the Germans enter our city. How can I possibly think of university, knowing that I might not live the next day, or even the next hour? But in the temporary safety of my parents' house, I am full of anger and rebellion.

The Nazis are not only killing us, they are depriving us of humanity, of our dignity as people. They are demonizing us, slowly, gradually, and with joyful malice. Do I not know it? And, if I do, am I able to articulate it? However I must know enough, instinctively, by not letting myself be paralyzed by fears. Instead, I escape into the pages of history where Carthaginians and Romans fight their heroic battles.

In the quiet times, my father says, "And this too shall pass." Then he adds, "What is all this against eternity?" But what if you are living a history in which there is a question of your death as the ultimate outcome? What then? How does one deal with one's own finiteness, especially as a teenager who is not streetwise?

I know now that I was escaping. I wanted to continue as long as it was possible as a human being with plans for the future. I knew, we all knew, that eventually Germany would be defeated. (I found out much later, from the pages of the Encyclopedia Britannica, that strategies deployed by Hannibal in his battles against Rome were copied in World War II.) If we could last long enough, we would be able to witness a page in history where a tyrant was destroyed.

So when my friend tells me about a teacher who is taking on students, I beg my parents to let me go. And they do. They must understand how important it is to feel normal instead of brooding in fear over an unknown and threatening end.

It is never safe for a Jew to go anywhere in the city, but especially so in the Jewish neighborhood where the ghetto is to be. The teacher lives in that area, and I go to her apartment to ask if she will take me on as a student. She agrees, even though I tell her that I can't pay for the time being, as we have no money.

For the next three months, I go to her house at least twice a week, if not every day. I do not get to pay her, and she never asks for anything. These are a glorious three months. She teaches me German, which I do not know. For a Jew it is dangerous not to know German. They assume that all of us know how to speak it. Should you say you do not understand it, anything can happen, from being roughed up to being disposed of.

My teacher also grills me on my French and introduces me to the rudiments of English. I can discuss anything with her, from my love of Gone With the Wind to my infatuation with Schiller's plays. I especially like Die Rauber, with its famous quotation, "Der Moor hat seine getan, der Moor kan gehen." Jugfrau von Orleans and Kabale und Liebe that I have seen in the theater. I can share with her my love of history and mythology. It seems to me that she has answers to all my questions. She seems to know it all. Of her apartment, I only remember the outlines of the austere room in which we meet, the two of us sitting across a striped tablecloth on a small wooden table.

I think we are both happy during these days, in spite of everything; in spite of hunger, in spite of sorrow, we have hope. At the end of the three months, a rumor spreads: there is to be a roundup. My mother immediately puts me on hold. A couple of weeks pass. Things are quieting down. To my joy, my mother prepares a bag of grits for me to give to my teacher. Happily I get on my way.

When I knock at the door of her apartment, there is no answer. The door is unlocked and I enter. Nobody is there. The place is empty. For a moment, I sit in this bare room at our small wooden table. Now I remember vaguely going out and trying to get information from her neighbors, from the passersby on the street. Nobody knows anything until one man says, "She might have been taken."

I go back to the open and abandoned study room and sit at the table with my little bag of grits, and I cry.

What did my teacher look like? I recall her in shades of brown and beige, brown hair, oval face, dark eyes, friendly, approving, and generous. What was she wearing? Probably something neutral: a dark skirt, a light-colored blouse. Nothing stands out in my fickle memory.

She has a special place in my mind and heart as an unsung hero among the heroes of resistance, of the ghetto days. At the risk to her life, she was a bearer of light and hope in the time of darkness and despair. It saddens me beyond belief that I do not remember her name.

THE HIDING PLACE | JANINE OBERROTMAN

I know that we were many in that room.

Of the strangers that were there,

I now remember only the mother with

the child in her arms and the bearded old man in the black hat. My mother and my cousins were in our party, Minna with her yellow-green complexion visibly denoting a kidney disease, and Irene with her kind face prematurely aged, with seven-year-old Dziunio, her son. Poor Dziunio. He could only whimper. Then another girl whose name, alas, I no longer remember. In the room, except for my people, we were strangers to one another.

Janine and her parents, "Moushka" and Maurice, in 1935.

Word went around that there was going to be a raid. We were all herded toward a side wall perpendicular to the window. In front of it stood a small buffet. As it was being pushed away, we saw a square opening at the bottom of the wall. We were told to crawl in. Once inside we heard the buffet pushed back into place, and then complete silence.

I realized that we were in a secret, closet-like space carved out of the dining room. Inside, we stood against a smooth, curved wall. The mother with the baby sat down, the child cradled against her breast. We breathed each other's air without a sound. The baby did not cry.

Light was coming from somewhere; I could distinguish shapes against the wall, the silhouette of the man in the black hat, the mother curled up over the baby. My cousins must have been on the other side of the curved wall. We were standing there, each with his or her thoughts. Nobody budged. My little cousin already knew how to be silent. I was next to my mother, as always, holding her hand. In my only-child's teenage heart, I knew that everything was all right as long as I could hold my mother's hand. Time passed. The baby still did not cry. It must have been drugged.

Suddenly we heard a familiar sound. Somebody was moving the buffet. It was too soon for the raid to end. We knew we had been discovered. Jewish policemen ordered us out. Some people were taken out immediately. The old man was taken first. I did not see the young mother again.

Our group was in the middle of the dining room when one of the policemen moved toward us. He singled out my mother and ordered her out. I froze. I suddenly noticed that her hair was graying. It had become disheveled in the turmoil of the hiding place. Had she turned gray overnight?

My mother objected vehemently. "I am young!" she cried out. My mother was forty-two-years old. The policeman did not insist and moved on. Did he take anyone else? I no longer saw anything as I clung to my mother. We were in the group left to wait. "For transportation," said the policeman.

After five hours he came back and said, "The contingent is filled. You can go free now."

Postscript: Had there been Gestapo, or Schutzpolitzei, or SS, or Ukrainian police in charge, nobody would ever have known what had happened there.

THE POTATO SILO | CIPORA KATZ

Cipora at six years old.

My uncle, Benjamin Feldman, appeared tall in my eyes, like a giant, although he was only five feet seven inches tall.

He was a strong man, strong like the Rock of Gibraltar, a man with an iron will. At the age of forty-one, he had charisma, determination, and courage. He was a leader with spiritual, physical, and emotional qualities. On a snowy November morning in 1942, he heard from Jewish leaders in the Semiatych ghetto in Poland, where we lived, that we all must flee at once. SS men and Polish police were circling the ghetto. Uncle Benjamin instructed his wife, Libby, to dress their four children, ages eight, ten, twelve, and fourteen, in warm clothes. He also told her to assemble the rest of our family: my father, Benjamin Fuchs, age thirty-two; my mother, Shifra, age thirty; me, Cipora, age four; and my grandfather and two aunts. We had all been living in the same ghetto for about eight months.

REFLECTION : SIMONA, MARTY, STEPHEN, ELI AND ZEV CITRON
(Daughter of Cipora Katz, and family)

Your hope for humanity resonates
in the whisper of the wind.
And when, on the grayest of days, the
sun emerges through the clouds,
we witness you triumph over darkness and despair.
In your memory we shall continue to
take a stand against intolerance, bigotry, and hatred.

You're never far from us as your
kind words, gentle touch, and warm smile
continue to perform miracles.
We will carry your message forward
and ask all to follow suit.
We will forever remember your love and light.

When we arrived at his house, my uncle gave each of us a package of sugar cubes. He explained that sugar, in times of hunger and thirst, could sustain an individual for some time, since every cube of sugar was about ten calories of carbohydrates. When my uncle told everyone that we needed to escape and why, my mother refused. She was waiting for my older sister, seven-year-old Bluma, to return home from visiting relatives in a nearby village. They were to follow us into the neighboring forests. My grandfather, Chaim Bash, also did not want to leave. He had to go to the synagogue to say Kaddish for his mother. He was very religious. My two aunts, Bashe and Kelle, went to be with friends in the ghetto.

My mother wrapped me in a light brown and beige wool blanket, about fifty inches by fifty inches, and handed me to my father to be held. Then we ran out of my uncle's house. Uncle Benjamin cut a hole in the wire fence that surrounded our ghetto and led our party of eight into the neighboring forest. From the years before the war, when he was a manager in a flour mill working with acquaintances who had farms in the forest, he was familiar with the area.

While we were running, we heard gunshots, but miraculously no one was hit. I recall a child crying in search of his mother, but we couldn't help. We did not even know our own fate, or if the child's mother was looking for him. As cold and windy as it got, my blanket was soft on my face and kept my tiny body warm. The blanket made me think of my mother and the rest of the family who were left behind. I was afraid, although my father hugged me tight. My eyes and blanket were wet from my tears. The blanket never came off of me; it was like a protective shield, holding my tears and my deep pain.

Uncle Benjamin now had to find a place to hide our party of eight, and with faith in God, he decided to look to his Polish acquaintances. He instructed all of us to pray and never give up hope. While we were hiding, he proceeded toward the farmhouse of a Polish acquaintance. Uncle Benjamin knew him because before the war he delivered milk from his farm to our family's summer cottage. He gave Uncle Benjamin a loaf of bread, but told him to move on quickly. The farmer was in fear for his and his family's lives. My uncle thanked him for the bread and returned to the area where we all were hiding.

Uncle Benjamin ran across other families in the forest. Some told him that his only hope of survival would be to travel alone, unencumbered by his family. My uncle said that he would survive with all of us or not at all. We continued to endure the cold and fear of leaving our tracks through the deep woods. Soon my uncle began his search for a temporary place to rest, deeper in the forest. In the distance he spotted a light. He decided to proceed alone toward it. He had a great premonition that this was a signal from God for him to follow. He arrived at a house. Looking in the window, he saw a woman weaving. He took a chance with his own life and knocked on the window. The woman crossed herself out of fear and asked my uncle what he wanted. He did not recognize her, but told her in what predicament he and his family were. She asked my uncle to come into the house and brought her husband into the room. As though it was a miracle from God, my uncle recognized him immediately as Mr. Luchinski, a Polish veterinarian indebted to my uncle for a past favor during the Russian occupation. My uncle reminded Mr. Luchinski of the time he had come to his flour mill pleading for flour to make bread for his family. All other flour mill managers had sent him away empty-handed. The economy was not good in Poland during that time.

Mr. Luchinski and his wife told my uncle to bring the entire family into their house. My uncle complimented Mr. Luchinski on his ability to save horses and livestock, and being chosen by God to save human beings. He left, and as tired as he was, reached the family in hiding and brought us to the Luchinskis' farmhouse. The Luchinskis told their own children never to divulge our whereabouts. It would endanger all of their lives.

Mr. and Mrs. Luchinski decided to hide us in their potato silo located not too far from the farmhouse. The silo was a hole below ground where potatoes were kept during the winter. It was covered with wood and branches with leaves. You could not see it at ground level, or from the air. My uncle explained to us that this was our only chance for survival.

The silo was small, and because of my size, I was the only one who could stand up. The rest of the family stood on their knees. It was a dark place. We only saw a ray of sun, or snowdrops, through the branches covering the silo. There was barely enough room to sleep, and we did so lying next to each other like sardines in a can, side by side. I was terrified, but I was too afraid to cry and be heard by German or Polish police patrolling the area. I learned that it was dangerous to cry, even as a four year old who was hungry, thirsty, or in pain. We held hands, prayed quietly in Yiddish or Hebrew, and counted each day of our survival on paper given to us by the Luchinski family. There were no games to play and no bedtime stories. I longed for my mother to hug me, but she was not with us. I had only my blanket to keep me company.

At night, my uncle looked for food for his family. He came out of the silo and went to the Luchinskis' farmhouse to pick up a pot of boiled potatoes and thin soup (which was like colored water) that Mrs. Luchinski prepared and left hidden outside the farmhouse. When my uncle returned, he divided the potatoes and soup into small portions among us, since it had to last for several days. My father would not drink the soup. He was very religious and had been studying to be a shochet, keeping strict kosher laws that prohibited him from eating certain types of food. My uncle tried to encourage him to eat, to save his life. As it is mentioned in Hebrew, "Pekuach nefesh doche hakol," the saving of life postpones everything.

After many days, weeks, and even months of suffering from hunger, thirst, and respiratory diseases, we began to regret leaving the ghetto. We questioned the fate of the rest of our family. We suffered from lack of sanitation. We were ridden with lice, and so was my blanket. Our only so-called toilet was a metal pot, like a helmet, and we used it for our bodily functions. When it was dark, my uncle took the metal pot out of the silo. He brought it deeper into the woods, dug out an opening in the ground under a tree, poured the body waste into the opening and covered it so that no one would see or smell it.

About one year after we entered the silo, under these horrible conditions, Mr. Luchinski's mother came to visit the Luchinskis. She was informed by Mr. Luchinski that they were hiding us. Out of pride, Mr. Luchinski's mother divulged this information to other grandchildren living close to the Luchinskis' farmhouse. Two of the grandchildren, ages sixteen and seventeen, entered our silo in the evening. They assumed that, since we were Jewish, we would have valuables. When they couldn't find anything, they beat my father and my uncle with their fists and left. Neither my father nor my uncle wanted to fight back and protect himself. They wanted to avoid making noise, and they were too weak. The two boys knew that what they had done would endanger their own family, so they kept quiet. That same evening, Mr. and Mrs. Luchinski found out about the attack and took us to their attic. We lay there as still as the dead, out of fear. At the same time, the German police came into their house for a routine search, but with God's help we weren't found. They knew that Mr. Luchinski was the only veterinarian in the area, so they made the search short. Several hours later we had to return to the silo.

Mr. Luchinski wanted to punish the two boys for what they had done. My family asked him not to do so. It would have brought on more problems. Mr. Luchinski, however, did tell them again that they had endangered their own family as well as us.

Uncle Benjamin, as strong as he was, became very sick after this episode. He suffered from a severe respiratory disease. It rendered him incapable of swallowing even a teaspoon of water. Late in the evening, when it was dark, Mr. Luchinski and his son carried my uncle to the farmhouse. With his medical knowledge, Mr. Luchinski applied glass blood suction cups to my uncle's back. In Yiddish we called them bunkes, heated glass cups to draw out infectious material, thus saving his life. He kept this routine up for ten days. Mr. Luchinski indicated that if Uncle Benjamin had died, he could not have kept us hidden anymore. My uncle was the leader of our group of eight.

After being in the silo for many months, my father died. I was five years old at the time. My family did not want to tell me. Thinking that he was asleep from being so sick, and unable to talk to me, I cuddled up to his body, covering him and myself with my blanket. I prayed quietly to God that my father would get better. I did not realize, even when I touched him, that since his skin was cold, he was dead. Because it was cold in the silo, we all had cold skin. And, because it was dark inside, I could not see the change in the color of his face. Now that I am a registered nurse, I know all of these signs and symptoms by touch and vision. My father lay with us, unburied, for seven days. The ground in the forest was too frozen for anyone to dig a grave. Late at night, Mr. Luchinski and his son poured boiling water on the forest ground until it softened. At the end of

Cipora, taken post-war in Israel (back row, fourth from the right).

seven days, when it was dark, my uncle and Mr. Luchinski took my father's body out of the silo and buried him by a tree deep in the forest. My uncle made a sign by the tree to mark the spot, vowing that, should he survive, he would return for my father's remains and rebury him in the Jewish cemetery in our town of Semiatych.

After my father was buried, I had a closer bond with my blanket. I spoke to it as if it was alive. I shared my sad and painful time with it. This partnership kept up for twenty-two months and three days in the silo. The Russian soldiers liberated us in 1944. By then we were like walking skeletons. Because we no longer had the energy to walk, the Russians helped us into one of their trucks.

The soldiers tried to feed us in small amounts, but because we had starved for so long, we vomited up the food. We proceeded with them toward the Russian border, at which time my uncle remembered the vow he had made when he buried my father by the tree. He decided to return to Semiatych. The soldiers wished us good luck, gave us some money, and helped us off the truck. In the area, my uncle noticed another Polish acquaintance with a horse and wagon. My uncle knew human character and was able to persuade the Pole to drive us all back to our home. For this good deed my uncle gave him some of the money we got from the Russian soldiers.

When we returned to Semiatych, we learned from Polish acquaintances who knew our family that my mother, sister, grandfather, aunts, uncles, and their children were taken to Treblinka. There they died, as we were told, on November 11, 1942, while we were in the silo. My heart ached, now as a six year old. I felt that I did not possess enough tears in my eyes as I cried for my parents and sister. I longed for them. I felt that I did not deserve to be punished. I had not misbehaved. As I got older, I did not even have the opportunity to visit their graves. I shared my pain with my blanket.

With the help of the Suchnut, the Jewish Agency, we slowly settled in, getting medical and physical help. When we became a little stronger, my uncle and his son, Shlomo, went back with a horse and wagon to the marked tree adjacent to the buried remains of my father. They recovered his body and took him back to Semiatych. They buried him in the Jewish cemetery, as my uncle had vowed to do. This cemetery no longer exists.

During our stay in Semiatych, for about six months, my uncle became our travel agent. He made plans, with the help of the Jewish Agency, for us to leave Poland and commence our trek to Israel. My Aunt Libby, two boy cousins, and I, along with my blanket, traveled to Romania. We were there for about five months in a kibbutz. Then we left for Israel, which was called Palestine at the time, and arrived in 1945. My uncle and his two daughters first went to Italy for one year, then Israel. We all settled in Petach-Tikva, "Gate of Hope." I finished my grammar school education at Bet Hasefer Levanot Netsach Israel, and continued for two years of high school in an agricultural school called Mikveh Israel. During my ten years in Israel, I made sure that my blanket was kept hidden and safe in a drawer.

During this time, my mother's uncle, Herman Bush, lived in the United States. After finding out that we had survived the Holocaust he came to see us in Israel. He decided to bring me to America. It took him seven years to get a visa for me. When I took the El Al plane to the United States, I had my blanket with me. We arrived on June 2, 1955.

From 1955 to March 2, 1995, no one touched my blanket. I kept it covered in a soft pillowcase in a drawer. Although I did not take it out, I always thought sadly about it. It was my link to the family I had lost in the Holocaust. On March 2, 1995, I showed this blanket as I was being interviewed for the Survivors of the Shoah Visual History Foundation, represented by Stephen Spielberg. At this time, my thirty-two-year-old daughter, Simona Shifra, saw my blanket for the first time. I had kept my painful past encapsulated deep in my heart, and this blanket was part of it. I did not want to inflict my pain on others. It was with the help of my daughter and my husband that I opened this capsule.

In 2006, I decided to donate my blanket to the new Holocaust Museum. I am the little girl who survived wrapped in the blanket. I wish it to be displayed as evidence of my family's suffering. This blanket is, to me, a treasure, an emotional memory that I will always carry deep in my heart.

We attribute our survival to Mr. Luchinski, God's help, and the true grit and determination of my uncle to stay alive. During my ten years in Israel, I never met a man as brave, dedicated to his family, or hard-working as my uncle Benjamin Feldman.

My uncle, who shared his wisdom, kindness, and strength with me, passed away in Israel at the age of seventy-eight, while I was in the United States. I regret not being able to attend his funeral, but I will always cherish his memory deep in my heart with all the righteous ones who went to heaven.

Father and mother, Benjamin and Shifra Fuchs, with father's family in 1931.

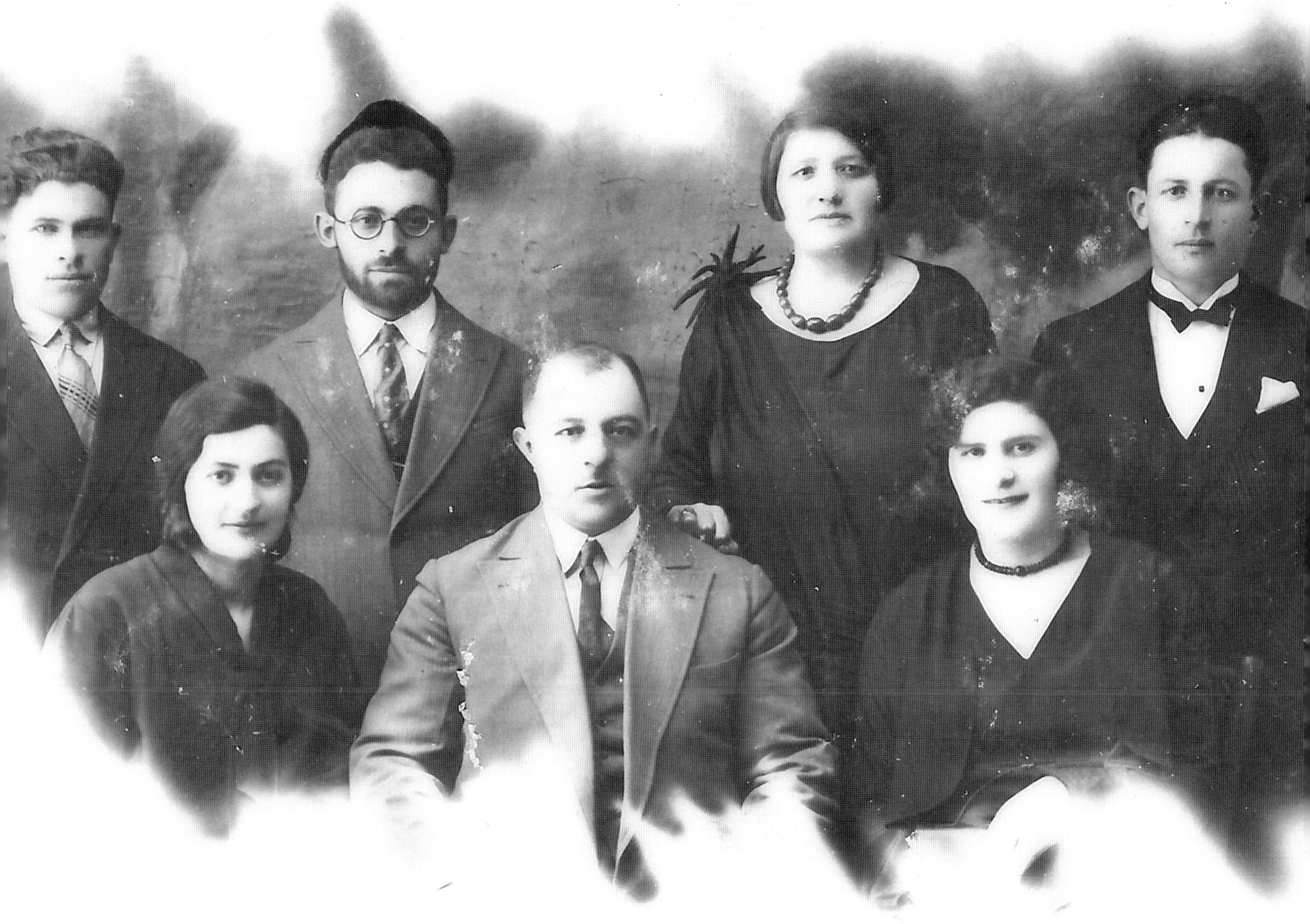

STORIES OF MY FAMILY | RALPH REHBOCK

Ralph, at four years old, on his mother Ruth's lap.

November 9, 1938
is known as Kristallnacht, "Night of the Broken Glass", or, in Germany, "the November Pogrom." The Nazis broke the windows of thousands of Jewish-owned shops. They burned over 1,000 synagogues. They picked up 30,000 men from their homes and sent them to concentration camps. Nazi rioters killed ninety-one men that night. My uncle, Salo Wahlhaus, was one of them. He was my mother's sister's husband.

REFLECTION : RALPH REHBOCK

If I only knew what would be happening to our family when I was a child of four. If I only knew how the actions of my gutsy mother were going to save us from possible extermination. If I only knew that a cousin in America was going to make it possible for us to leave my country of birth and German language and happy early childhood.

In 1933, the Nazis took a census and knew exactly where the 500,000 Jews in Germany lived. Jews had registered when Hitler and his democratically-elected government ordered them to do so. On that night in November, they were intending to arrest Salo along with other Jewish men under the age of sixty. No women, no children under the age of sixteen, and no men over sixty were taken.

The Nazi soldiers knew where my father lived, but he was not at home that night. He never went home again. My uncle, Salo, was at home that night. The Nazis came to his apartment in Gersfeld.

Uncle Salo had been severely wounded during World War I and could hardly walk. He was on a disability pension from the German government. Nevertheless, the Nazis told him to come with them. He showed them his documents, yet they still ordered him, "Come with us."

He explained to them that he couldn't walk. They insisted, but he didn't move fast enough. Finally, they kicked him down the stairs of his house. When his wife, Renny, found him, he lay dead at the bottom of the stairs.

Aunt Renny called my grandfather for help. Grandpa came to bury his son-in-law. At this time the non-Jewish gravediggers were not permitted to bury the Jewish dead anymore. It had become the family's responsibility to do the burying. Grandpa enlisted the help of a Polish man whom he knew. They hired a horse and wagon and moved Salo to the cemetery.

It became evident from that day on that life in Germany would be devastating for the Jews. If only my Aunt Renny and others would have been convinced that they should try to leave. After the events of Kristallnacht, my parents knew that we had no choice but to arrange for our escape. This required assistance from our family in America. We were fortunate to find cousins who were willing and able to make this happen.

In December 1938, my parents knew that there was no chance for the life we had enjoyed before to ever return. They decided that we would leave Germany. My father escaped in early December by sneaking onto an airplane at the Berlin Airport, a plane that he knew was scheduled to go to London where his uncle was living. He would be safe.

My mother and I had waited for months for approval to leave. My mother had gathered together all of the necessary papers, and she had packed and shipped all of the household and personal belongings that we were allowed to take. This included some of my favorite toys and books. My father had once purchased a classic train set for us to take to America. It was a 00 gauge Marklin train set, including a passenger engine with six scale model cars and a freight engine with eleven cars. They were authentic and able to run on an elaborate array of tracks with stations, bridges, crossing gates, lamp posts, passengers, luggage, and many other pieces.

My favorite building block set was also carefully packed for shipping. It included a number of parts with detailed instructions and floor plans drawn to scale for houses, churches, and stores to build. There were columns, windows, roof shingles, doors, clocks, and bricks. I could build real looking miniature structures.

All that was left to be done was for Mother and me to get to England to join my father in time for us to board the ship, the SS Manhattan, and sail from Southampton to New York, USA.

Mother and I got on a train in our hometown of Gotha, Germany on December 15, 1938. We were heading toward the boat train that would take us across the English Channel. This means of transportation no longer exists. It was a ferry on which whole trains crossed the Channel. We would first have to cross Germany and then Holland.

As we arrived at the German-Dutch border, we were ordered off the train along with the other Jewish passengers. The train station at the border was typical of European stations of the 1930s, a main building with ticket sellers and waiting rooms. People were coming and going, but we were kept isolated from the non-Jewish travelers. The Nazis strip-searched us to determine that we weren't carrying any forbidden items, such as jewelry, loose jewels, or money in excess of the ten marks that we were allowed to take out of the country.

The Nazi soldiers told us to get dressed and wait for the next train. Suddenly, as we stood with the others, a total stranger came up to my mother and tapped her on the shoulder. He spoke in a low voice. "When I give you a signal," he said, "take your little boy and run with me."

Where would he be taking us? A short time later he moved his hand toward his cap. This was the signal that he had given my mother to expect. He started to run and we followed. He was heading for the German-Dutch border. He knew the exact moment when a local train was to leave the station on a track that was in Holland, which was then still a free country. We jumped onto the train with him.

What would have happened to us if we had not run with the stranger? Would the train that the guards told us to wait for have taken us to one of the concentration camps? Would we have been stuck in Germany and not allowed to emigrate to the United States?

We don't know who the stranger was or why he did what he did. Was he Jewish or Gentile? Did he do this once, for us only, or did he do this multiple times to help others escape from Nazi Germany. We were taken to his home and were able to place a phone call to my grandmother in Gotha. Then, Oma Clara called her brother in London, to tell my father that we were all right and would be arriving in England later than he expected. The stranger had saved our lives.

My Mother, Ruth, died on March 8, 2000. We went through her belongings and we found a letter hidden in her underwear drawer. It was written on January 10, 1943 by her sister, Renny. She wrote the letter to my mother as a final farewell. She knew that she and her son were destined for a concentration camp and certain death.

In 1938 cousins living in the United States offered to help Aunt Renny and her six-year-old son, Alfred, to leave Germany, but she did not want to go. She chose to stay, as so many other German Jews did. They thought that the Nazi regime would go away. She moved to Berlin after leaving her original home in Gersfeld, Germany when her husband, Salo, was killed during Kristallnacht in 1938. The family was religious and lived as Orthodox Jews. My aunt felt that she and Alfred could no longer live safely in her hometown, Gersfeld, and moved to Berlin to seek work and refuge.

Renny had made contact with several non-Jewish families to protect and hide her in their homes in Berlin. With her typing skills, Renny found work as a secretary. Records show that she lived at three different addresses in Berlin.

The Groll family made sure that Renny and Alfred had meat to eat by sending something by messenger each week to Berlin, where they were being hidden. The Grolls owned the butcher shop in Ohrdruf. They were friends of my grandfather, who was a cattle dealer in the town and sold meat to the Grolls' store.

The Marx and Michaelis families gave Renny and Alfred places to live in Berlin and cared for Alfred so that Renny could work. We did not know anything about these families until Renny wrote of them in the 1943 letter to my mother.

In 1942, the Nazis began the Final Solution.

Trying to hide had become more and more difficult and dangerous for both the Jews in hiding and those who were hiding them. On January 10, 1943, Renny heard a siren wailing outside in the street. She knew that when the vehicles stopped, the sirens stopped. A police van was in front of the house where Renny and Alfred were hiding. Since Renny was a secretary, she had very fast typing skills. She dashed off a letter and secretly hid it where the owners of the house could find it.

My Dearly Beloved!

It is hard for me to write this letter of Good-bye to you. You will get it from your friends. It is not possible to send it myself anymore. Our situation is more than tragic. I had thought Alfred and I would see you again, but other plans have been made for us. But, try anyway to find us. Maybe God is watching over us. My last wish is that you do as many good things for the Family Groll as you have the ability to do. They took such good care of us and it is only because of their help that made it possible for us to stay alive, until we have to leave. They cared for us as only parents do for their children. Do as much as you can. I know that you will fulfill my last wish because it is my request to you. Also, be very good to and take care of Willy and Alma Marx because they were brave, true and very devoted to us and did what they could. Please see if you can find Mr. and Mrs. Dr Michaelis. Maybe they will have the luck to live through this. They are extra good people and have always taken good care of us and gave us a home with them. They raised Alfred and took care of him because I had to work. They deserve only the best.

I thank you for everything and have only the best wishes for you. Stay well! Don't forget us. I will think of you until my last hour.

Everything good for your lives. I kiss you in my heart and will love you until my death.

Yours,
Loving you with all my heart,
Renny

Frau Michaelis found the letter and managed to send it to America, where they knew my mother to be living at that time. My mother got the letter with my aunt's wedding ring enclosed in the envelope. The letter told of the people who had helped her to survive to that time. She would be thinking of her family, as she wrote, "until my last hour." She knew she was going to die. "Other plans have been made for us."

My mother must have received this letter sometime after the war ended in 1945. By 2000, so much time had elapsed. We had no idea as to the details and logistics of Renny and Alfred's experiences after Uncle Salo's death in 1938. It was impossible to find any of the protecting families more than fifty years later.

She and Alfred were taken to Auschwitz on the 33rd Transport Train. They were both killed in the gas chamber on March 3, 1943. We know this date because the Nazis kept meticulous, detailed records of all those who were imprisoned and killed. We found the specific record of Renny and Alfred's deaths in Israel at Yad Vashem, the Holocaust Memorial, in 1988. Our family had gathered for the celebration of a cousin's bat mitzvah. The cousin was one of Renny's great granddaughters. Her grandmother, Helaine, was Renny and Salo's daughter. She had been sent to America to live with cousins, the Max Schrayer family, in 1937, when Jewish school-aged children were no longer allowed to attend school in Germany. Helaine was twelve years old at the time, and was ultimately adopted by the Schrayer family after the Renny's death was officially verified. The Schrayer family was also responsible for saving my parents and me by sponsoring our United States visa in 1938.

ONE DAY AT CAMP STUTTHOF | MARGIE OPPENHEIMER

It was Sunday, August 6, 1944. We were herded like animals onto a ship, overcrowded, no place to sit, to lie down or even to use the bathroom. I was pushed into a corner with a lot of life preservers. There I sat, all by myself and did not move.

I had a glimpse of hope that maybe my mother or my brother would be on the ship as well. Suddenly, someone called my name. With all the noise and commotion it was a miracle that I heard it. A lady saw me and gave me horrible news. My mom had been picked at the last roll call where everyone over thirty and under eighteen was picked. By now we all knew that this meant extermination. What else could go wrong? My brother was saved at this time, though he was not yet eighteen. He had to finish a job he was assigned to do by the SS. I hoped that this news would be wrong and that one day we would meet again.

House and parents' storefront on Lange Strase 45, where Margie grew up.

REFLECTION : MARGIE OPPENHEIMER

Embrace the opportunity for education. Education was something I was robbed of. I feel strongly that it not only empowers a person to better their chances of success in life, but also provides a sense of pride and equality.

The journey took three long days and nights. At one point I tried desperately to get to the bathroom. We all longed for a breath of fresh air or a drink of water. The lines, as you can imagine, were endless. I made it halfway up the stairs when I was kicked from behind and pushed back down the stairs with the usual, "A Jew has no will, he only has to feel pain." I was not able to use the bathroom. I will never forget that kick. It pierced me. I stayed still, alone in that corner with the life preservers. I did my business there. I am sure I was not the only one to take this measure. The stench of urine and feces was unbearable in the awful heat. I am sure that many people died under these terrible, cruel conditions.

It was a blessing to smell fresh air again after we were finally unloaded and released. We were in the port of Danzig, Germany, on the Baltic coast. At this point we were allowed to rest on the grass. Fresh air and sunshine truly felt wonderful. No water or food yet. After a while, in this peaceful place, we were once again herded toward the water into very small boats. We were one hundred people on a boat designed for fifty. I was certain we would drown. At this point I was despondent. I did not care if I lived or died. There was also a terrible thunderstorm. The water was very choppy and the boat was jerking around from one side to the other, but it was still on the water. After a long stormy night, suddenly all was calm, and the boat stood still. We heard roaring voices, "Everyone out. Out with you, faster, faster." We were all so weak and worn and could barely stand on our feet. But with rubber clubs and rifle butts we were beaten out of the boats. Anyone who could not stand up or walk was shot on the spot.

We were chased like this for about five kilometers, mostly through a wooded area. We reached a place called Waldlager Forest Camp, beautiful, cozy little houses with curtains on the windows. Little flower gardens gave them the look a youth hostel. Of course, these were not for us, but for our commanders, dignitaries, and guards. No one would have guessed what was behind this peaceful area just a short distance away.

We marched right past it, not too much further, but far enough to be out of sight for any visitors, until we reached a big gate. We walked through the gate into Stutthof concentration camp, surrounded by high-voltage, barbed-wire fences. Men and women were separated. As always, we were herded like animals into the barracks; three people to a bunk, three tiers high. The hustle and bustle and shoving, as usual, was intolerable. At six in the morning we heard a whistle. "Everyone up. Quick, hurry up, faster, faster, roll-call." Roll call was in between barracks, and as usual, it took about two hours. Afterward, we hoped to be able to go to sleep or at least try. No food or water yet. We all got weaker and weaker. So ended our first day.

Three in the morning. A wake-up call. "Everyone up. Faster! Faster! Roll-call." The water had been turned off, so using the bathroom was also out of the question. The roll call lasted two hours. Then our commander started to count all of us once again, lasting another two hours. If we thought that was it, we stood longer to wait until our barracks were cleaned. Finally, after several long hours of standing for roll call, we each had to pass by our brutal block elder, a woman Kapo who was a political prisoner herself, and in charge of us, the Jewish captives. As we marched by her, we would get a ladle of coffee, one slice of bread with either a teaspoon of butter or jelly. When everything had been given out, we were once again chased out of the barracks. If we were not fast enough, we would be beaten with the rubber club. If, by any chance, we were able to reach the bathroom, we would find that the water was again turned off. This is the way we spent most of our days in Camp Stutthof.

Here we did not work, either, but were introduced to something new: lice. Our only occupation was catching these new invaders. Like monkeys we sat, whenever there were no roll calls, trying to catch them and kill them. However, it seemed the more we killed, the more would come back. You had to kill the eggs, which we often missed.

Once, I saw my Aunt Lucy in another barrack behind an electric barbed wire fence. When my Kapo saw me, she beat me with a rubber club and told me, "Talking to other prisoners is forbidden. If I catch you again, I will kill you." I had talked to my aunt for just one moment but never saw her again. We assumed that she did not survive. She did not return to our hometown.

Under these conditions I survived my time in Stutthof. Then, we had a different roll call. This was not in between the barracks, but in a great wide field where we had to undress and march, stark naked. My fear took over. I thought our time for extermination had come. It was what happened when these sorts of killings took place. People had to undress to their bare skin, line up in front of previously prepared trenches, and get shot by machine gun. Then, they would drop into the trenches. However, I did not see any trenches here. Instead, we had to form a large circle, and march past the commander in charge, with all the dignitaries and guards surrounding us with their hateful grins. We had to listen to their individual remarks, which were grotesque and hurtful and always ending with the four famous words, "You, to the left!" or, "You, to the right!" This was the way we were inspected for work, just like the cattle dealer offering his cattle to the highest bidder. If we were sent to the right, we were okay for work and escaped death. Work was like a certificate for life. I was ordered to the left with about five hundred older-looking women. I was chased to another barracks away from the people I had met in my previous one. I was very small, very weak, very thin, and had a Roman numeral II marked on my left forearm. This meant that I was unable and unfit to work. I knew my time had come.

This was by far the most humiliating, embarrassing, degrading, and worst day. In the evening, I looked across the fence to the other side when I suddenly noticed two of my old friends from Meteor, the rubber factory in Riga where I had worked before our transfer to Stutthof. They also saw me and walked toward me. Without any words spoken between us, we all knew what we had to do next. I swiftly fell to the ground in front of them and the electric-loaded barbed wire fence and carefully they pulled me to the other side. I was so malnourished that I never touched the fence. It was a miracle that no one saw us and that no one reported us. Fanny and her cousin, Rosaly, saved me from the pit of death. Today, I believe, it was God who gave us the courage and strength to pull this miracle off. I removed one of the Roman numeral I's on my left arm and then found a place to sleep on the floor.

Six in the morning roll call, everyone out, faster, and avoid the club. Roll call again was to count everyone. Once more I panicked. I was standing behind a tall person and did get counted. At the end there was one person too many. "Who is the person that does not belong here? Come forward now!" I tried very hard to remain calm and stay put behind the tall person. Again and again the commander yelled to come forward. My face felt like it was on fire, and if it had been noticed everyone would have known I was the person. Finally the commander gave up, and chose an elderly-looking person to send to the other side. For a moment I felt relieved, but then I felt very guilty. Guilty for being selfish and saving my own life, for sending another innocent person to her death. This guilty feeling possesses me to this very day, as I relive this most horrible experience of all my camp days.

A few days later, I was picked for an outside commando with both of my true and loyal friends, Fanny and Rosaly. We were picked for hard labor construction in a labor camp in Sophianwalde in Pomerania, eastern Germany.

Oppy working for the American Joint Distribution Company in 1947-48.

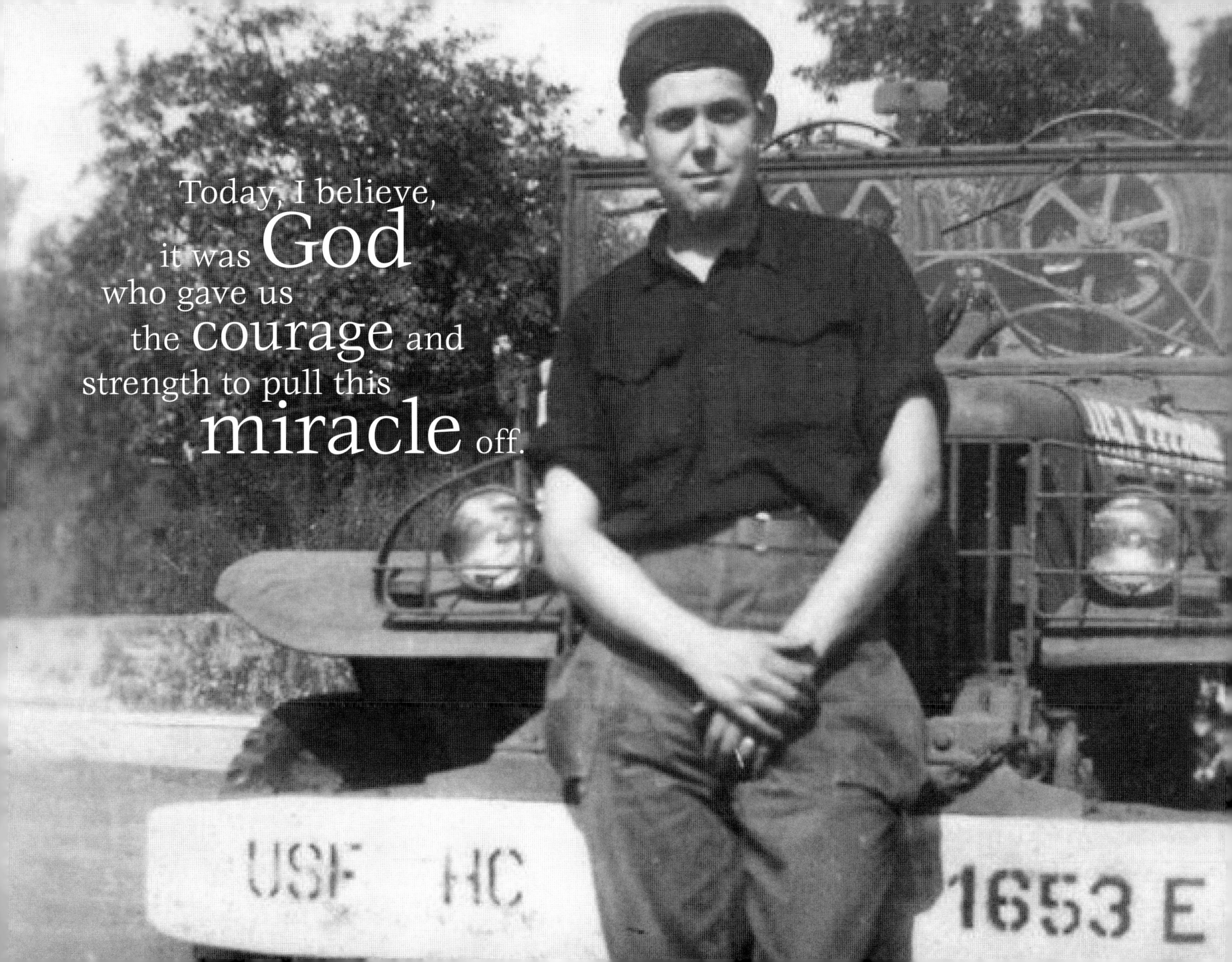

Today, I believe, it was **God** who gave us the **courage** and strength to pull this **miracle** off.

OPPY | MARGIE OPPENHEIMER

Who was Oppy?

I hadn't heard of him until a woman from my hometown came to my place of work and asked for him. I worked for the American Jewish Joint Distribution Committee (AJDC) in Frankfurt (Main), Germany. It was housed in a big building with many different departments. I worked in the emigration department with Ellen. She was the third person, besides my brother and I, liberated from the camps to return to our hometown. Oppy supposedly worked for the AJDC. So Ellen and I went to every department, but the answer everywhere was the same, "Sorry, we've never heard of him." We had one more place to check out, the dispatcher. Finally, "Yes, you'll find him in the back working on one of our trucks." I walked with Ellen to the backyard and called out his name. When I saw him walking toward us, I left Ellen and went back to work. Now I knew there was a man named Oppy.

Lotte, Margie and brother Jochen.

Some time later, a young man walked into our office and asked if I could help him emigrate to America. I asked if he had any relatives or friends there. He answered, "My name is Oppy and I have no one." I stared at him and was startled for a moment, but proceeded to fill out his application. He appeared to be a very nice young man, tall and very slender with dark hair and big dark eyes.

Many years ago, when society played a different role than it does today, it was a crime for a young girl of fifteen or sixteen years old to become pregnant. She would be thrown out of her house, left to fend for herself and treated with contempt. Oppy's mother, Erna, only fifteen, went for a walk in her parents' garden. She was very developed for her age. She had a strong build, with broad shoulders and long, pitch-black curls and big dark eyes. It was a warm, sunny spring day when her parents' gardener accosted her and sexually assaulted her.

She had been brought up very strictly. Going on dates at this age would be out of the question. When Erna's parents found out what had happened, they made her leave the house and support herself. It was a shande, a disgrace, for a Jewish girl like Erna to get into this situation. Erna, all of fifteen, went through her pregnancy alone and delivered a baby boy on January 4, 1926. She named him Herbert Joachim Oppenheimer. She left the baby at the Jewish Orphanage in Berlin Weissensee, where she eventually worked as a baby and infant nurse.

Emil and Hedwig Gall came to the orphanage looking for a foster child. They walked through rows and rows of baby cribs until they came to the very last crib, all the way in the corner. Here was a baby crying. Hedwig said, "I want this baby," but was told, "You don't want this one. He is a Jewish child." Hedwig and Emil both insisted. His tiny neck was sore and red from crying. Soon after Hedwig cuddled him, he stopped.

The Galls carried him home, still in Hedwig's arms. All seemed happy and content. They didn't change anything in his name, but called him Little Herbie. The Galls were not Jewish, but Seventh Day Adventists, very religious and strict in their beliefs. They celebrated Saturday as their day of rest. Their services were also on Saturday. Their dietary laws were very similar to the Jewish ones. Women could not wear make up. Seventh Day Adventists could not go dancing and also refrained from drinking alcoholic beverages.

Little Herbie was raised in the Galls' faith. They were not wealthy. Emil worked as a house painter and made enough money to provide food, shelter, and clothes for the three of them. When they brought Little Herbie home from the orphanage, he didn't even have a bed or crib as yet, but he had lots of love. He was placed into a box padded with blankets and pillows to keep him warm. This special box was placed behind the kitchen table on a bench. Besides the kitchen they had a bedroom-living room. He didn't lack anything.

When the Galls took Little Herbie to the doctor for the first time, they were told he would not reach three months of age. He had a bad case of asthma. Three months came and went. Herbie celebrated his first birthday and many after that. He proved the doctors wrong. Herbie was a happy baby. He grew bigger and Emil built him a beautiful new bed that was also placed behind the kitchen table and served as a daybed during the day.

Eventually Erna found out where her baby had gone. She looked up the Gall family and paid them a visit. The Galls welcomed her with open arms and she was so grateful to find her baby healthy and taken care of with love and compassion. She visited regularly and often and was introduced to Little Herbie as "Aunt Erna."

When Herbie was six and of school age, he went to a public school and did well. He made friends and was liked very much. One day, he didn't come home after school and Hedwig became worried. So many things could have happened, especially being a Jewish child. Until now he had been saved from the atrocities that were happening everywhere due to the Hitler regime. A friend of Herbie's came to tell the Galls that he had fallen and couldn't walk. Emil ran as fast as he could to find his boy on a hill unable to get up or walk. Emil picked him up and carried him to the nearest hospital. There the doctors found that he had fractured his femur, but was otherwise in good health. The bone was set, and he had to stay in the hospital for a little while. He healed well. After some time he was able to come home, go back to school, and continue his usual activities. When Herbie returned to school, his friends thought of giving him a nickname. His name was long and difficult, so they now called him "Oppy." Everyone liked the name and he kept it.

After twelve years, Oppy's life suddenly came crashing down. Because of Hitler's regime, the sweet, caring Hedwig and Emil could no longer take care of their boy. They had been told numerous times to give up the boy or go to jail. Before they let him go, he was told that Aunt Erna was really his biological mother. Oppy, Hedwig, and Emil embraced. Over the years Oppy and Erna had become very fond of each other, but now the true love showed. The good-bye to Hedwig and Emil, though, was very sad and emotional.

Although he was temporarily sent to the Jewish orphanage in Berlin Weissensee, where he soon became a bar mitzvah, Oppy knew deep in his heart that this was not the last he would see of his beloved foster parents. On weekends, when he had free time, he visited Hedwig and Emil. He also met with his mother, Erna, who had become a loyal friend to the Gall family.

Oppy's stay at the orphanage wasn't long, and when he became a teenager he was sent to several different Jewish foster homes. Unfortunately these stays were very short. Jews were emigrating, or, caught in Hitler's web and sent to the concentration camps. Oppy enrolled in the ORT School, a Jewish entity. ORT stands for "Organization of Educational Resources and Technical Training." Founded in 1880, it was a trade school open to young people. (Today there are ORT schools all over the world, even one in Chicago, the Zarem Golde School.) Oppy was trained as a typesetter. He still visited Hedwig and Emil for as long as he could. His mother's visits had become a bit more difficult as she went underground and lived under an assumed name. She stayed in touch as much as possible. She worked now for a dentist.

Oppy was sent to Auschwitz. At sixteen he was alone for the first time, without his foster parents. They had raised him and tried to protect him from this very new and cruel world. But he felt alone now, even though there were many thousands of people around him.

First day in Auschwitz: "Hurry up and stay in line!" they shouted again and again. Then a shot, a man fell down, his head split open. Oppy prayed, "Dear G-d, don't let them kill me yet." He heard the Shema Yisrael. This was the beginning of a totally new and cruel life. He was chased into the barracks, "Hurry up, faster, faster!" Finding an unoccupied place was another ordeal.

Oppy learned fast. He knew that to survive he had to follow orders. He met two young men who had also come from Berlin. They became friends and spent two years interned at Auschwitz. They stuck together and helped each other in any way they could. All three found odd jobs inside the camp until they were transferred to another camp. They traveled to this camp partially by train, but mostly they walked, what they called the death march. The walk was especially hard for Oppy, as he had some big, open, painful sores on his legs. His two friends, Hans and John, helped him, and at times dragged him along. Finally, after a gruesome and long march, they arrived at Mauthausen concentration camp. There they tried to get some medical help for Oppy but were not successful.

Margie with her mother and Lotte in their garden in 1935.

Mauthausen was a camp like any other camp. Conditions were the same: overcrowded barracks, daily role calls. At meal times you had to be fast, as often there was not enough food for all of the inmates. Luckily their stay wasn't too long. They were liberated on May 5, 1945.

Oppy was in very poor health, very weak, and in terrible pain. John went to one Russian officer and told him about Oppy. He was immediately taken to a makeshift hospital where he was cleaned, given nourishment and medical care. He was then sent to a hospital in town. The Russians nursed Oppy back to good health.

After a few weeks, he was reunited with his two friends, who had waited for his recuperation. As Oppy, Hans, and John got strong enough, they tried to make their way back to Berlin. This, of course, was quite difficult. It took a long time. The war was over but life was not back to normal yet. Transportation was very poor, almost nonexistent. The three tried to hop trains whenever possible. If they got on to a train, they would only go a short distance because the tracks had been bombed. When there were no trains, they roamed the streets trying to find food and shelter. At larger cities they tried to find help from churches or medical organizations. Finally, they made it to Berlin where the three split up. Each one lived in a different area, but they all promised to stay in touch.

In Berlin, Oppy found the house where he was raised still in good condition. He walked up the stairs and knocked on the door. Hedwig opened it. "Oh my G-d! Emil, come look! I can't believe it! Our boy! Is it really you? Is it not a dream?" she cried. "Please, boy, come in! Look at you! You are just skin and bones and not a boy anymore. You are a young man."

The reunion was emotional and overwhelming. "Sit down, my boy, come, sit down," Hedwig said. "I knew you'd come back. Look, I show you." She presented a picture of Oppy in a frame, which she had hung on the wall with just a thread. "I knew that as long as the thread holds the picture, you are alive, and come back. And here you are." Tears were on everyone's faces.

After the first excitement died down, Oppy asked about his mother. The news was not so good, but for the moment they put it aside. It was a happy day for all three of them. When Oppy told of his experiences they all got somber, but were grateful he had come back alive. He stayed here for a little while. His next goal was to find out about his mother, Erna. The dentist for whom Erna had worked said that the last time he had seen Erna was on January 5, 1945. She was going to visit Hedwig and Emil that evening but never showed up. That day there had been a very bad air strike, and many people had lost their lives. Oppy also tried to find out if there was any chance Erna had been found and sent to a camp. Unfortunately, everywhere he checked, the answers were all negative. Erna must have died alone, just as she had been at fifteen. He left word with the dentist, that if he heard anything, to let him know. He also spoke to Hedwig and Emil and explained that he didn't see the possibility of a life for him in bombed-out Berlin. He would go west. So once again, Oppy headed for the road.

He knew it would not be easy, but he tried. He felt he must have still had the help of Ha-Shem on his side. He made it to Frankfurt(Main), a bigger city in the middle of Germany. The American army was stationed there. Oppy registered at the city hall and was assigned a room with a very nice family. He then applied for a job at the American army base. He had a room now, a job that earned him a little money, and meals, too.

At first he worked in the kitchen, though he did not speak English. One day he was sent to the storeroom, to get some grease. Gries in German, spelled differently, but pronounced the same, is farina, so that is what he looked for. Everyone started laughing and thought it was funny. They explained to Oppy what they really wanted and helped him with the English language.

He worked as a helper wherever help was needed. At one point his sergeant wanted him to empty out a garage and told him to get some German guys to help him. Oppy saw some auto tires and asked Sergeant Gomez if he could take them home. The sergeant answered, "Anything you like you can take." So he took the tires. He thought his landlord might be able to use them. The German fellows reported him to the police who came to arrest Oppy. They told him to get a lawyer. Oppy replied, "I don't need a lawyer. I had permission from Sergeant Gomez." When the police tried to check it out, they had a problem finding the sergeant. He had suddenly been transferred. Oppy had to spend some days in jail and now had a record.

After this episode he didn't go back to work at the American army base, but thanked them for giving him the opportunity to work. He started to work for the AJDC where he stayed for several years. He was hired as a driver, but also did minor repairs on the cars. Major repairs went to the auto repair shop. After work and on most weekends he had the car at his disposal.

It was here that I met Oppy, that day when he came to the office where I worked, the emigration department, and asked my help with an application to emigrate. I filled out his application and started him on his way. We, and some other young people who worked there, soon became friends. Most of them were also registered to emigrate. Oppy sometimes drove dignitaries like President Eisenhower, and once or twice Eleanor Roosevelt. Hanne, Eva, Oppy, and I often took our off days and weekends together. Oppy was able to drive us, and we took some nice trips into the countryside.

Oppy and I became very close, and, after a two-year courtship, we married in 1949 and started a family. Together, we waited for our turn to immigrate to the United States. It seemed to take forever. On September 9, 1953 we finally arrived in Chicago. It was Rosh Hashanah, the Jewish New Year. "A new year, a new beginning, a new life." We were blessed with thirty plus years here as free people and were able to make a new life after the Holocaust. Oppy passed away in 1990.

The war was over but life was not back to normal yet.

Margie's wedding photograph in January 17, 1949.

AUSTRALIA BOUND | MARGIE OPPENHEIMER

My husband

Oppy, our daughter Ruth, and I left Frankfurt (Main), Germany at the end of October 1951. We boarded a train going to Genoa, Italy. Arriving in Genoa, we were assigned a room in a hotel until our departure, about two days later. Things are not so easy when you don't speak the language. I don't want to complain, because we were happy to come this far.

Family photograph — Front: Lotte, Margie and her mother. Back: her father and Amy holding Jochen.

The people at the hotel didn't understand when I asked for warm milk for our baby. No interpreter was available. So I was sent to the kitchen. I couldn't believe what I saw: in a huge kitchen, wall-to-wall roaches. I couldn't understand how people could work there and we, the customers, eat there. It was awful. I walked out backwards and forgot about getting the warm milk. I couldn't wait till our departure. I told my husband and we were very careful about what we ate. Actually, the rest of the hotel was very clean. We couldn't complain. Nor did we want to be ungrateful. The International Refugee Organization had paid for our journey and the stay at the hotel.

We boarded the boat on Sunday, the last day of October or the first day of November. The tables were set for lunch, very clean and festive with white tablecloths. My daughter and I were assigned a cabin. All men were separated as they were assigned to the quarters of the crew. The crew had to share the luggage area. On the dining room tables, I saw some green fruit appearing to be grapes. I tried to eat one and noticed it did not taste like a grape. I got sick immediately, before the boat even took off. What I had tried to eat was an olive, which I had never seen before. Oppy thought that it was very funny. I didn't think so, for I was really sick. But I recuperated soon, though I couldn't eat lunch or dinner that day.

Our boat was not a luxury liner, but a converted cargo Ship. Many people complained. After about two or three days we arrived at the Suez Canal, Port Said. We had to pass an inspection. While that was going on, there were many merchants trying to sell their goods. It was quite interesting. After an all clear, we were on our journey to Australia. For many weeks we saw only water and sky. Sometimes the boat just stood still, for one or another repair. The complaints got worse. Our journey was to last only two weeks, but that had passed already, and the journey was really taking six long weeks. There was some entertainment, a swimming pool, a movie theater, some deck games, and so on. Mostly, we had time to take it easy.

One time, the boat stood still again. The captain decided that it had too much of an overload, and had the crew throw crates of food overboard to alleviate the weight. We could get off the boat when we came to any port. We saw Ceylon and Bombay, two very interesting places. We passed the equator, no port, but we had a big party on the boat for this occasion, lots of food and drink and entertainment. Many people got drunk. Oppy took pictures.

We soon came to ports in shorter intervals. Finally we arrived at our first Australian port, the city of Perth. What a very pretty, quaint place, looking very European. From here our next port was Melbourne, lots of industry, damp and foggy. We didn't spend much time here. Oppy got quite sick with a bad asthma attack and we returned to the boat. Oppy was put in sick bay. I didn't see him for the rest of the journey, not knowing if he was dead or alive.

On Saturday, December 15, we arrived in Sydney, our destination. It was a beautiful summer day. Ruth, my daughter, and I got on deck very early to see the most beautiful sunrise and the sights, when suddenly Oppy appeared, all smiles, all better. It was like a miracle.

We were met by members of the Jewish community and assigned to a hostel with many more refugees, all new immigrants. We had room and board. It was a new experience for us. There were people from all over the world.

Oppy found a job immediately in a service station very close by. His coworkers had lots of fun with his poor English and his pronunciation. After a while, I also found a job, which I did from our one-room apartment. I was taping paper covers for phonograph records. I delivered a finished job on Friday and started again on Monday. After I delivered my work, I proceeded to clean our room for the weekend. I threw out all the scraps and accidentally picked up the negatives from the pictures Oppy took and discarded them, too. We didn't notice this until Oppy was ready to develop them and couldn't find them. He was very upset, but not more than I was for being so careless.

We stayed at the hostel for a while, until we found a room with a family. The landlady had originally come from Berlin but had lived in Australia for some time. She was quite helpful to us. We found a nursery school for our daughter, and I found a job, too. My first one was in a chocolate factory. I couldn't take the smell of chocolate all day long and looked for something else. I then started to work in a laundry, where I stayed. I learned to iron a shirt in seven minutes. We were in Sydney for nineteen months. We met many people I knew from the time I spent in the Riga ghetto, where I had been sent first from Germany. They all were making a good living in Australia, but we still hoped to be able to go to the United States.

In June 1953, we were called to the American consulate where our emigration to America was approved. By September of that year we had our visas. Without any further problems we were finally on our way. We left Sydney on September 9 on a British airline. Our first stop was Fiji Island. We flew by night and arrived in Hawaii, also on September 9. We had a few hours stop there and flew again, by night, to San Francisco. From there, finally, by eight in the evening, we arrived at Chicago's Midway airport where my brother and sister-in-law met us. After all this time, we were finally in America.

Margie and Lotte in Stettin in 1930.

It was a new experience for us.

BIOGRAPHIES

SIA HERTSBERG

is a Holocaust Survivor who, at the age of forty-eight, came from Latvia to the United States in 1975. She learned to speak and write English here. With the help of Benita Haberman and Matthew Sackel she has been able to write stories for this book. Sia currently resides in Glenview, Illinois.

FELA DOGADKO

was born in Warsaw, Poland and traveled throughout the Soviet Union to escape the Holocaust. She has written about this journey in honor of her mother, who carried the responsibility of their survival with uncompromising dignity, great wisdom, and unwavering optimism. Fela currently resides in Chicago, Illinois.

PETER GERSHANOV
NOV. 7, 1932 – JULY 9, 2014

with his mother and brother, came to this country in 1946 to join his father. He learned English by speaking it and no other language at home. After completing high school, he received a BS in Engineering from Illinois Institute of Technology and served as a First Lieutenant in the United States Air Force. He went on to complete an MBA at Northwestern University. The exercise of writing his life stories has brought him through a time he had not considered in the last sixty years.

JOE KOENIG

was born in Czestochowa, Poland. He came to the United States as a teenager in 1952 and graduated from Lakeview High School in Chicago. He currently lives in Skokie, Illinois and has six grandchildren.

JANINE OBERROTMAN

survived the initial German occupation of Poland by hiding with her family inside and outside the Lvov ghetto. In 1943 her mother and aunt helped her to escape, take on a Polish identity, and move to the country. After being denounced, she was jailed and deported to Stuttgart, Germany to do forced labor. After Liberation she went to Paris. Eventually, in 1953, she and her husband and son settled in the United States, where she had a career as a teacher and counselor in the Chicago area.

Bio Photos: Deja Views

JULY 10, 1938 – SEPT. 18, 2014

CIPORA KATZ

settled in Israel after the war when she was a girl. In 1955 she arrived in the United States at the age of sixteen. From then on she knew she wanted to be a nurse. She achieved this in 1961. Cipora donated several objects to the Museum, including the wool blanket she wrote of in her story.

RALPH REHBOCK

was born in 1934 in Gotha, Germany. A cousin helped him and his family to come to the United States after Kristallnacht in 1938. He currently lives in Northbrook, Illinois and is retired.

MARGIE OPPENHEIMER

was born in Germany. Married to another Holocaust Survivor, she initially went to Australia after the war and came to the United States in 1953. She is a retired nurse in Skokie, Illinois and works as a volunteer for the C.J.E. Senior Life program. She is thankful for a "far better life than I could have ever imagined."

MATTHEW SACKEL

is the Education Coordinator for the Illinois Holocaust Museum and Education Center. He is responsible for, among other things, the photographs in this book. He graduated with his Masters in Library and Information Science from Kent State University. Matthew is also responsible for the development of the Brill Family Resource Center, the Museum's Library.

ESTHER YIN-LING SPODEK

is the writing coach for the Survivors' Writing Workshop at the Illinois Holocaust Museum and Education Center. She has an MFA in Creative Writing from Indiana University and an MA in History from Northwestern University. She is a teacher, editor, and writer in the Chicago area, where she lives with her husband and two sons.

EPILOGUE | MATTHEW SACKEL

On January 2, 2008, I started working for the Illinois Holocaust Museum and Education Center as the Museum's first librarian. My initial assignment: to work with a newly formed writers' workshop made up of Survivors who met once a month at the Skokie Public Library. I was to serve as both a staff liaison and an editor for a publication we hoped to create.

This room full of strangers was about to embark on a journey of trust, collaboration, and hard work. Each session included readings by the authors and then a roundtable brainstorming session. Someone walking past the room might have wondered what we were doing that could inspire both laughter and tears.

I was lucky to work one-on-one with the authors, typing up their stories as they spoke. I learned new words in foreign languages, scanned dozens of photographs, and listened to the stories behind each one, all the while gaining a whole new perspective on what it meant to have lived through this incredibly difficult period in time. At the end there were no strangers in the room; all those months of hard work resulted in the first *In Our Voices*.

This second edition includes some new material and editorial corrections, and honors two of the authors who are no longer with us. It has been a pleasure working with all of the authors, and our staff and survivors are excited to share the updated *In Our Voices, II*.

~ February 2016

ILLINOIS HOLOCAUST MUSEUM
& EDUCATION CENTER

BOOK DESIGN

Jason Star designed the cover and interior layout of *In Our Voices, II : Stories of Holocaust Survivors*. ITC Veljovic was the selected font used in the body of the book and displays an obvious calligraphic heritage. The creator of the serif face, Jovica Veljovic, was strongly influenced by German designer Hermann Zapf and Israeli designer Henri Friedlander. Henri Friedlander (born 1930) is an American historian of the Holocaust noted for his arguments in favor of broadening the scope of victims of the Holocaust.

ACKNOWLEDGEMENTS

Carrying out a project like this takes many people who provide many forms of support. We would like to thank our families for giving us some of the reasons for writing our stories. We thank the Skokie Public Library for providing us with a place to meet and discuss. We would also like to acknowledge the generosity of Northern Trust Bank in the funding of the first publication of this book.

This book has been generously published by

This book has been generously funded by

Northern Trust